Encyclopedia of the NFL

NFL

VOLUME ONE: Aikman, Troy >> Guard

By James Buckley, Jr.
Jim Gigliotti
Matt Marini
John Wiebusch

KEY TO SYMBOLS

Throughout *The Child's World® Encyclopedia of the NFL*, you'll see these symbols. They'll give you a quick clue pointing to each entry's subject.

Active Coach **Active Player** **Football Term** **Hall of Fame** **Miscellaneous** **Stadium** **Super Bowl** **Team**

The Child's World
www.childsworld.com

Published in the United States of America by The Child's World®
1980 Lookout Drive, Mankato, MN 56003-1705
800-599-READ • www.childsworld.com

ACKNOWLEDGMENTS

The Child's World®: Mary Berendes, Publishing Director

Produced by Shoreline Publishing Group LLC
President / Editorial Director: James Buckley, Jr.
Designer: Tom Carling, carlingdesign.com
Assistant Editors: Jim Gigliotti, Matt Marini

Interior Photo Credits:
AP/Wide World: 6, 9, 11, 23, 24, 27, 29, 41, 44, 45, 48, 53, 54, 64, 75, 79, 81, 91, 94, 97, 103;
Corbis: 18, 66, 98; Getty Images: 20. All other images provided by Focus on Football.
Icons created by Robert Pizzo.

LIBRARY OF CONGRESS CATALOG-IN-PUBLICATION DATA

The Child's World encyclopedia of the NFL / by James Buckley, Jr. ... [et al.].
  p. cm.
Includes index.
ISBN 978-1-59296-922-7 (v. 1 : alk. paper) – ISBN 978-1-59296-923-4 (v. 2 : alk. paper)
– ISBN 978-1-59296-924-1 (v. 3 : alk. paper) – ISBN 978-1-59296-925-8 (v. 4 : alk. paper)
 1. National Football League–Encyclopedias, Juvenile. 2. Football–United States–Encyclopedias, Juvenile.
I. Buckley, James, 1963– II. Child's World (Firm) III. Title: Encyclopedia of the NFL.
  GV955.5.N35C55 2007
  796.332'64--dc22
                              2007005662

■ Lou "The Toe" Groza

S INCE ITS FOUNDING IN 1920, THE National Football League has played more than 12,000 games in 100 U.S. cities—and 10 countries. More than 17,000 players have strapped on their pads. They've combined to put up more than 400,000 points and score more than 45,000 touchdowns. That, my friends, is an awful lot of football!

In *The Child's World® Encyclopedia of the NFL*, we won't have room to include all of those players or recount all of those touchdowns. But we've put our helmets together and tried to give a complete picture of the very best and most important people, places, teams, and terms that football fans like you want to know more about.

You'll meet great members of the Pro Football Hall of Fame and read about today's top players. You'll relive some of the NFL's most memorable moments—from the Sneaker Game to the Coldest Game to the Greatest Game Ever Played. Need to learn how to "talk football"? These books will help you understand the terms and phrases you'll hear during a game. Finally, each of the NFL's 32 teams is covered with a complete history. All you'll need to enjoy these books is a love of football . . . and a knowledge of the alphabet!

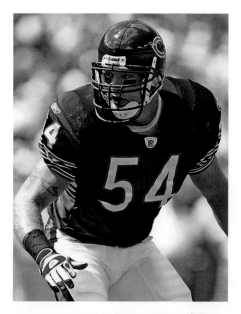

■ Chicago Bears (Brian Urlacher)

Contents: Volume 1: Aikman, Troy >> Guard

Aikman, Troy

A former number-one NFL draft choice and a Super Bowl MVP, quarterback Troy Aikman was inducted into the Pro Football Hall of Fame in his first year of eligibility in 2006 (former players must wait five seasons before they can be nominated).

Aikman, whom Dallas chose out of UCLA with the top pick in 1989, went on to play all of his 12 NFL seasons with the Cowboys. An inspiring leader, he often sacrificed personal glory for the good of the team, and did not post the big statistics of many of his peers. Still, he made the Pro

■ *Troy Aikman led the Cowboys to three titles.*

Bowl five times, and his 32,942 passing yards and 165 touchdown passes are Cowboys' career records. More importantly, he led Dallas to three Super Bowl wins in a four-year span in the 1990s. He was named the MVP after passing for 273 yards in the Cowboys' 52-17 rout of Buffalo to cap the 1992 season.

Since retiring following the 2000 season, Aikman has worked as an analyst for NFL games on television. He also teamed with former Dallas quarterback Roger Staubach on ownership of a stock-car racing team that competes on the NASCAR circuit.

Akron Pros

A charter member of the NFL in 1920, the Akron Pros were named the league's first champions after going 8–0–3 that season. Though no official standings were kept in 1920, the Pros were the only NFL team to go undefeated, and they were awarded the league title at an NFL meeting in April of 1921.

One of the stars in the Pros' first season was running back Fritz Pollard, who was one of only two African-Americans to play in the league that year (it was not until 1946 that the color barrier officially was shattered). One year later, Pollard became the NFL's first African-American coach when he was named co-coach of the Pros along with Elgie Tobin.

Akron went 8–3–1 in 1921 and finished in third place in the league. But the Pros had just one more winning season after that. They went out of business following a 1–4–3 season in 1926.

All-America Football Conference

One of the more successful of various challengers to the NFL over the years, the All-America Football Conference had a short life (1946–49), but a lasting impact

Alexander, Shaun

A touchdown machine, running back Shaun Alexander set an NFL record (since broken) by reaching the end zone 28 times in 2005. While doing so, he also helped the Seattle Seahawks reach the Super Bowl for the first time.

A 5-11, 225-pound back, he has both the size to make him hard to tackle and the speed to outrun defenders. The former Alabama star spent 2000, his rookie season, backing up Ricky Watters. Alexander became the primary starter in 2001 and gained 1,318 yards on the ground.

But he first made national headlines in a prime-time, Sunday-night game against the Minnesota Vikings early in the 2002 season. That night, he gained 231 yards from scrimmage (rushing and receiving) and scored five touchdowns in the first two quarters of Seattle's 48–23 victory. It marked the first time in NFL history that a player scored five TDs in a single half.

By then, scoring touchdowns was quickly becoming Alexander's specialty. After equaling the club record with 16 scores in 2001,

■ *Alexander is one of the NFL's top scorers.*

he broke the mark by reaching the end zone 18 times in 2002, then set another standard with 20 touchdowns in 2004 before his monster season in 2005.

Meanwhile, Alexander also is rapidly moving up the NFL's rushing charts, and is closing in on the all-time top 20. His 1,880 yards in 2005 marked a career high and his fifth consecutive season of more than 1,000 yards. He is also the Seahawks' career rushing yardage leader.

Allen, George

George Allen was a master motivator who never had a losing season in 12 years as an NFL head coach. That in itself is noteworthy. Even more remarkable, Allen built his record despite taking over two franchises that had been mired in losing ways often before his arrival.

Allen was the defensive coordinator for the Chicago Bears before the Rams hired him for his first head-coaching job in 1966. Los Angeles had lost more games than it won for six consecutive seasons before then. But Allen's first team went 8–6. The next year, the Rams went 11–1–2 and won a division championship.

In 1971, Allen signed on to coach the Redskins, who were coming off a 6–8 season. They had just one winning record in 15 years, and hadn't played in the postseason since 1945. But Allen took Washington to the playoffs in his first season in the nation's capital, earning a wild-card berth with a 9–4–1 record. The next year, the Redskins went 11–3 and won the NFC East.

Allen's Washington teams were known as the "Over-the-Hill Gang" because he liked to rely on older players instead of youngsters. He liked to trade draft choices and young players for veterans that other teams felt were past their prime. Given the general-manager duties in Washington as well as the head-coaching job, he immediately traded for veterans such as quarterback Billy Kilmer, wide receiver Roy Jefferson, linebacker Jack Pardee, and others. They played key roles as Washington advanced to Super Bowl VII in the 1972 season. In all, the Redskins reached the postseason five times in Allen's seven seasons as coach.

When Allen stepped down at Washington following the 1977 season, he had a career record of 118–54–5 (including postseason games). At the time, he ranked 10th among all-time NFL coaches in victories. He still has the third-best winning percentage (.686).

Allen later came out of retirement to coach in the United States Football League, and was the head coach at Long Beach (California) State when he died at age 72 in 1990. He was inducted into the Pro Football Hall of Fame in 2002.

■ *Coach George Allen.*

on pro football. That's primarily because of the later success of the Cleveland Browns and the San Francisco 49ers—two former AAFC teams—but also for other several other new ideas.

The AAFC first introduced many of legendary Browns coach Paul Brown's ideas to pro football. The league also was the first truly national league, with multiple teams on the West Coast several years before the NFL had more than one team in those markets. It also helped integrate pro football with the addition of African-American players in 1946 (the NFL also did so the same year). Such innovations helped the new league eat into the ticket sales and media attention of the established NFL.

The Browns won all four AAFC championships and perhaps sped the end of the league with their dominance as fans in other cities lost interest. (Cleveland was so strong that it also went on to win the title its first year in the NFL in 1950.) The Browns, 49ers, and Baltimore Colts—not the same Colts' franchise still in existence—as well as various individual players awarded to NFL teams, were incorporated into the NFL when the AAFC shut down in December of 1949.

Allen, Larry

Versatile Larry Allen has proved to be one of the premier offensive linemen in the NFL during a lengthy career that

■ *Big Larry Allen takes up a lot of space!*

began in Dallas in 1994. After signing with the 49ers as a free agent in 2006, Allen made the Pro Bowl for the 11th time in his 13 NFL seasons.

The 10th overall pick in 1994 out of Sonoma State—no player from the Division II school ever had been drafted before—the 6-3, 325-pound Allen was pressed into duty almost immediately, starting 10 games while playing both guard and tackle his rookie year. By the next season, he was a full-time starter at guard, and he made the Pro Bowl while playing for the Cowboys' Super Bowl champions. Over the next decade, he played each guard and each tackle position for Dallas. He became only the third player in NFL history (after Bruce Matthews and Chris Hinton) to earn Pro Bowl honors at more than one position along the offensive line during his career.

■ *Marcus Allen first starred for the Raiders.*

Allen, Marcus

A former Heisman Trophy winner at the University of Southern California, running back Marcus Allen had little trouble building on his collegiate success in the NFL, where he enjoyed a stellar 16-year career from 1982 to 1997. In that time, he established himself as one of the top rushing-receiving threats in league history, and he exhibited a nose for the goal line.

The 10th overall selection of the Raiders in the 1982 draft, Allen began his pro career playing on the same field—the Los Angeles Memorial Coliseum—as he did in college. He was the NFL's top rookie in '82 after scoring a league-leading 14 touchdowns in just nine games of the strike-shortened season. The next year, he ran for more than 1,000 yards (1,014) for the first of three consecutive seasons and helped the Raiders reach Super Bowl XVII against Washington. In that game, Allen burned the Redskins for 191 rushing yards (a Super Bowl record at the time) and put an exclamation point on the Raiders' 38-9 victory with a 74-yard touchdown run on the last play of the third quarter.

Two years later, Allen rushed for a career-best 1,759 yards. He and the Raiders eventually had a falling out, however, and his playing time dropped. After the 1992 season, he joined the rival Chiefs.

Late in his second season in Kansas City in 1994, Allen went over the 10,000-yard rushing mark for his career. The next season, he topped 5,000 career receiving yards, and thus became the first player in NFL history to reach both of those plateaus.

Allen's career total of 12,243 rushing yards ranks 10th on the NFL's all-time list. His 123 rushing touchdowns rank second in league history only to Emmitt Smith's 164.

Alley-Oop Pass

The "Alley-Oop" was the nickname given to a play made famous by the San Francisco 49ers and their 6-foot 3-inch

Alworth, Lance

Perhaps the greatest wide receiver in American Football League (AFL) history, Lance Alworth caught 542 passes in 11 seasons from 1962 to 1972. He was inducted into the Pro Football Hall of Fame in 1978.

Alworth played nine seasons with the San Diego Chargers before finishing his career with two years in Dallas. He was nicknamed "Bambi"—a label he didn't particularly like. But it was based on the ease and grace with which he roamed through opposing defenses. His sure hands and blazing speed helped him to average 18.9 yards per catch and to grab 85 touchdown tosses during his career.

■ *Alworth was a 1960s AFL star.*

Alworth was an AFL all-star from 1963 to 1969. He led the AFL in receptions, receiving yards, and touchdown catches three times each. With their star wide receiver as the cornerstone of a powerful offense, San Diego reached the AFL title game three consecutive seasons in the mid-1960s, winning once.

In 1965, Alworth helped the Chargers reach the championship game by averaging a whopping 23.2 yards on his 69 catches. He topped the AFL that year with 1,602 receiving yards and 14 touchdown catches, both of which turned out to be career bests.

When Alworth was voted to the Pro Football Hall of Fame, he was considered the first true AFL player to make it in.

pass-catching end R.C. Owens in the late 1950s.

Owens, a former college hoops player who was a rookie in 1957, would set up in the end zone, basketball-style, then out-jump smaller defensive backs for a lob pass from quarterback Y.A. Tittle. The first time the pair tried it, they teamed on an 11-yard touchdown pass late in the fourth quarter to beat the rival Rams 23–20. Several

weeks later, they did it again, combining on a 41-yard touchdown pass in the final seconds for a dramatic 35–31 victory over the Lions.

The Alley-Oop, which was named after a famous comic-strip character of the time, was a precursor to today's "Hail Mary" passes in which a tall receiver tries to out-jump defenders for a high-arcing desperation throw.

Alltel Stadium

The home of the Jacksonville Jaguars since the inception of the franchise in 1995, Alltel Stadium was built on the site of the old Gator Bowl stadium.

In 1994, builders tore down all but the west upper deck of the Gator Bowl's stands, then worked feverishly to complete the new stadium in a record 19 1/2 months in order to open in time for the Jaguars' expansion season. The stadium has an official seating capacity of 67,164, though more than 78,125 fans witnessed the Patriots' 24–21 victory over the Eagles in Super Bowl XXXIX there in February of 2005 (several sections of seats are covered with tarp for regular-season games).

Alltel, which purchased naming rights to the stadium, is a telecommunications company that provides wireless services to customers in dozens of states.

American Bowls

As part of a major effort to expand its fan base around the globe, the NFL began playing a series of international preseason games called American Bowls in 1986. In the first American Bowl game, the defending Super Bowl-champion Chicago Bears beat the Dallas Cowboys 17–6 at London's historic Wembley Stadium.

Since then, the NFL has played 39 more American Bowls in a dozen cities around the world. Atlanta's 27–21 victory over Indianapolis in August of 2005 marked the 40th American Bowl game, and the 12th to be played in Tokyo, Japan.

The NFL has played as many as four American Bowls in a single season. There were no American Bowls scheduled for 2006.

American Football Conference (AFC)

The American Football Conference (AFC) was born following the AFL-NFL merger that took effect before the 1970 season. The 10 former franchises of the AFL (see American Football League, 1960–69) were joined by three existing NFL franchises—the Baltimore (now Indianapolis) Colts, Cleveland Browns, and Pittsburgh Steelers—in the 13-team AFC. The remaining 13 NFL teams were placed in the National Football Conference (NFC), with both groups playing under the NFL banner.

In subsequent years (1976, 1995, 1999, and 2002), the league added expansion franchises to bring its total number of teams to 32, with 16 in each conference.

American Football League (1926, 1936–37, 1940–41)

Before the American Football League of the 1960s gained a foothold in pro football, three earlier versions of the AFL tried to compete with the NFL. They were

American Football League (1960–69)

The American Football League of the 1960s successfully challenged the established National Football League, producing a merger that resulted in the shape the NFL retains today.

When prospective owners of a half-dozen franchises met in Chicago in the summer of 1959, they were dubbed the "Foolish Club" for the absurd notion that they could compete with the NFL. By then, the NFL had clearly established itself as a major sports league after nearly four decades in existence.

But two months before the AFL kicked off play in eight cities (see chart, page 12), the league signed a five-year contract with ABC to televise its games. That gave the new league a financial strength that previous competing leagues did not have, and it gave the new enterprise nationwide exposure. With the battle lines drawn, the AFL waged war on the NFL for the next several years, holding its own draft and offering enticing bonuses to big-name stars. The biggest was former Alabama quarterback Joe Namath, who refused an opportunity to play in the NFL by signing a record $400,000 contract with the AFL's New York Jets on New Year's Day in 1965.

Finally, in June of 1966, the competing leagues reached a settlement. Under the terms of the merger, the existing AFL teams all would join the NFL and would begin playing a common schedule in 1970. They also formed the American and National Football Conferences. The leagues also agreed to have their two league winner meet beginning in 1967 in a world championship game, which has since come to be known as the Super Bowl.

■ *The Buffalo Bills celebrated after winning the 1964 AFL title.*

all called AFL but only the one that started in 1960 lasted very long at all.

The first of the early AFLs began in 1926. It had perhaps the best collection of talent of the competing leagues. Its star attraction was famous halfback Red Grange, though the league featured several other former NFL stars as well. One was Johnny Scott, who led the Philadelphia Quakers to the league championship that year. Grange, who played for the Chicago Bears fresh out of college in 1925, had helped save the NFL at the gate the previous season. But he jumped to the AFL's New York Yankees in 1926. Though the nine-team league didn't survive, Grange's Yankees were admitted into the NFL for the 1927 season.

Two more AFLs came along in the late 1930s and early 1940s, each initially featuring just six franchises. But each league folded after its second season. The lack of success by rival leagues proved the staying power of the original NFL.

Andersen, Morten

A left-footed kicker with a booming leg, Morten Andersen the NFL's all-time leading scorer with 2,445 points (through 2006) during a lengthy career. His 24 playing seasons rank second only to Hall of Fame quarterback and kicker George Blanda's 26 years.

Andersen was born in Struer, Denmark, but moved to the United States when he was a youngster. New Orleans drafted him out of Michigan State in the fourth round in 1982. In 13 seasons with the Saints, he made the Pro Bowl six times. He went on to play for Atlanta, the New York Giants, Kansas City, and Minnesota before retiring following the 2004 season. Early in the 2006 season, the Falcons talked him into returning to the team for another season, at the age of 46!

Andersen's 540 career field goals and his 40 career field goals of 50 yards or more are the most ever.

THE ORIGINAL AMERICAN FOOTBALL LEAGUE (1960)

Eastern Conference

Buffalo Bills

Boston Patriots

Houston Oilers

New York Titans
• The Titans changed their name to the Jets in 1963.

Western Conference

Dallas Texans
• Dallas moved to Kansas City and became the Chiefs in 1963.

Denver Broncos

Los Angeles Chargers
Los Angeles moved to San Diego in 1961.

Oakland Raiders
• The AFL also added expansion teams in Miami (1966) and Cincinnati (1968).

Anderson, Gary

Kicker Gary Anderson is second on the NFL's all-time scoring list, with 2,434 points scored during a 23-season career.

Anderson, a native of South Africa and a graduate of Syracuse University, was a steady, if unspectacular, kicker for the Pittsburgh Steelers (1982-1994), Philadelphia Eagles (1995-96) and San Francisco 49ers (1997) for more than a decade. But his career surged after he joined the high-scoring Minnesota Vikings in 1998. That year, he became the first kicker in NFL history to make all of his attempts in a regular season—35 field goals and 59 extra points—and his 164 total points were the most ever without the benefit of a touchdown. Unfortunately, he also is remembered for a key field-goal miss in the Vikings' NFC title game loss to Atlanta that year.

Anderson went on to play four more seasons for the Vikings and two with Tennessee before retiring at age 45 following the 2004 season. George Blanda (26 years) and Morten Andersen (24 years) are the only players with more playing seasons.

■ *Danish native Morten Andersen starred for five different NFL teams.*

Anderson, Willie

Cincinnati's Willie Anderson is one of the biggest (6 feet 5, 340 pounds) and best (four consecutive Pro Bowl selections entering the 2007 season) offensive linemen in the NFL today.

The 10th overall pick of the 1996 draft out of Auburn, Anderson stepped into the Bengals' starting lineup for the final 10 games of his rookie season and has been a mainstay ever since. He helped pave

continued on page 16

13

Arizona Cardinals

The Arizona Cardinals are the oldest franchise in the NFL, with roots that date back more than two decades before the league began play. But even with more than 100 years of history, the club has had little success. The Cardinals have won only two NFL championships, and they once went 51 years between postseason victories.

Arizona plays in the West Division of the National Football Conference (NFC). The Cardinals joined the St. Louis Rams, San Francisco 49ers, and Seattle Seahawks in the West when the NFL realigned into eight divisions of four teams in 2002. Before that, the Cardinals had played in the NFC East since the AFL-NFL merger took effect in 1970.

The Cardinals are the oldest continuously run pro football franchise in the nation. They began as a neighborhood team in Chicago in 1898, when the city's Morgan Athletic Club started playing football. Shortly after the turn of the century, owner Chris O'Brien bought some uniforms secondhand from the University of Chicago. But the university's maroon uniforms had faded over time. When he saw them, O'Brien said, "That's not maroon. It's cardinal red!" Thus, the franchise got its nickname.

The Cardinals were one of 14 teams to play in the NFL's first season in 1920. They were called the Racine Cardinals that year after a street that bordered their home field. By 1921, though, they were called the Chicago Cardinals. The franchise remained in Chicago through 1959 before moving

■ *Charley Trippi was a Cardinals' star in the 1940s.*

■ *Quarterback Matt Leinart led the Cardinals in 2006.*

Cardinals. He achieved legendary status when he intercepted a pass with casts on both hands to protect broken fingers. In the 1970s, quarterback Jim Hart guided a high-powered offense named "Air Coryell" after head coach Don Coryell. In the 1990s, local college star Jake "The Snake" Plummer was drafted out of Arizona State University.

But postseason appearances have been rare. The 1925 Cardinals were named NFL champions with a record 11–2–1. In 1947, the Cardinals won their only NFL Championship Game, beating Philadelphia 28–21. Coryell helped the team reach the playoffs in back-to-back seasons in the mid-1970s. But a wild-card playoff win over the Cowboys in 1998 was the only postseason victory since the 1947 title game.

For 2006, the Cardinals added Pro Bowl running back Edgerrin James and former USC star Matt Leinart at QB. He threw to a pair of talented youngsters in Anquan Boldin and Larry Fitzgerald at wide receiver. In addition, the team moved into their new stadium.

to St. Louis. In 1988, the club moved again, this time to Phoenix. They were known as the Phoenix Cardinals until 1994, when they became the Arizona Cardinals.

Over the years, the Cardinals have featured many colorful characters and excellent players. In 1929, fullback Ernie Nevers scored all of the Cardinals' points in a 40–6 rout of the Bears on Thanksgiving Day. That still stands as the NFL record for points by a single player in a game. In the late 1940s, the club featured the "Dream Backfield" anchored by halfback Charley Trippi. In 1960, safety Larry Wilson began a Pro Football Hall of Fame career with the

---

ARIZONA CARDINALS

CONFERENCE: NFC

DIVISION: WEST

TEAM COLORS: CARDINAL RED, BLACK, AND WHITE

STADIUM (CAPACITY): UNIVERSITY OF PHOENIX STADIUM (63,400)

ALL-TIME RECORD: 458–664–39

NFL CHAMPIONSHIPS (MOST RECENT): 2 (1947)

the way for nine 1,000-yard rushers in Cincinnati's backfield in his first 10 seasons as a full-time starter (entering 2007). That includes Rudi Johnson's club-record 1,458 yards in 2005.

An excellent pass protector as well as a run blocker, Anderson and his offensive linemates surrendered only 21 sacks in 2005. It was the lowest single-season total in club history.

Arrowhead Stadium

Arrowhead Stadium has hosted Kansas City Chiefs' home games since opening in 1972. It combines with neighboring Kauffman Stadium, the home of baseball's Kansas City Royals, to form the Harry S Truman Sports Complex.

Every Chiefs' home game since the 1991 season has been sold out at the 79,451-seat football-only stadium, giving the club a decided home-field advantage over its opponents. That helped Kansas City forge the NFL's best regular-season home record during the decade of the 1990s. The Chiefs won 65 of their 80 games at Arrowhead from 1990 to 1999 and reached the playoffs seven times.

Assistant Coaches

Every NFL head coach relies on a staff of assistants to help create game plans, offer instruction during practice, and act as a link between him and the players.

■ *A sea of red: A packed Arrowhead Stadium cheers the Chiefs to many home victories.*

As late as the 1950s, many staffs consisted of just an offensive assistant and a defensive assistant. But as specialization increased on the field, it did on coaching staffs, too. All teams now employ separate assistants to coordinate the offense, defense, and special teams. They also have assistants for each position within the offense and defense, plus a strength and conditioning coach. Many teams also have assistant head coaches and quality-control coaches, and some assistants even have assistants!

In 2006, the Denver Broncos employed the league's largest staff. The Broncos had 20 assistants working under the head coach that season.

Associated Press NFL MVP Award

Unlike other major sports, the NFL does not award an official most valuable player trophy each season. But the Associated Press' annual winner has unofficially come to be recognized as the most prestigious of the NFL MVP awards handed out by various media outlets.

Cleveland Browns running back Jim Brown earned the first AP NFL MVP award after leading the league in rushing as a rookie in 1957. Brown, who also won the award in his final NFL season in 1965, was the first two-time winner. Green Bay quarterback Brett Favre (1995, 1996, and tied with running back Barry Sanders in 1997) is the only three-time winner.

■ *Vince Young works with an assistant coach.*

Only four defensive players have won the award, the last being New York Giants linebacker Lawrence Taylor in 1986. Washington Redskins kicker Mark Moseley (1982) is the only specialist to win it.

Astrodome

The Houston Oilers played in the Astrodome from 1968 until moving to Tennessee following the 1996 season.

Originally dubbed the "Eighth Wonder of the World" because it was the world's first multipurpose, domed stadium, the Astrodome began hosting Houston Astros baseball games in 1965. The builders originally tried to grow grass inside the dome.

■ *The Houston Astrodome was the first indoor stadium. Many others have been built since.*

When that failed, scientists developed a new brand of synthetic turf: AstroTurf.

During the Oilers' heyday of the late 1980s under head coach Jerry Glanville, Houston fans and the media called the Astrodome the "House of Pain" because of the hard-hitting defenses that helped the club reach the playoffs three consecutive seasons.

Atlanta Falcons

Please see pages 20-21.

Atlanta–Fulton County Stadium

Atlanta-Fulton County Stadium was the home of the Atlanta Falcons from the inception of the franchise in 1966

until the club moved into the new Georgia Dome in time for the 1992 season.

In 1978, the stadium hosted two of the most memorable games in club history. Late that season, Steve Bartkowski's desperation, 57-yard touchdown heave to Alfred Jackson in the final seconds lifted the Falcons to a stunning, 20–17 victory over the Saints. One month later, in the first postseason game in club history, Bartkowski passed for two touchdowns in the final five minutes to rally the Falcons to a 14–13 victory over the Eagles.

The multipurpose stadium also hosted Atlanta Braves baseball games from 1966 to 1996, and earned the nickname "The Launching Pad" because of the many home runs hit there. It was the sight of Hank Aaron's historic 715th career home run in 1974, the blast that broke Babe Ruth's long-standing major-league record.

Attendance

The NFL set a league record when 17,340,879 fans attended its 256 regular-season games in 2006. That's an average of 67,738 fans per game. In 2005, the largest crowd to see an NFL regular-season game saw Arizona's 31–14 victory over San Francisco. The attendance of 103,467 at Azteca Stadium in Mexico City, Mexico. It was the first regular-season NFL game outside of the United States.

The largest crowd ever to see any NFL game also was at Azteca Stadium, when 112,376 fans watched the Cowboys and Oilers play a pre-season game in 1994.

The largest crowd to witness a Super Bowl came on January 20, 1980, at the Rose Bowl in Pasadena, California. The Steelers beat the Rams 31–19 in Super Bowl XIV that day before 103,985 people.

Audible

When a quarterback changes the play at the line of scrimmage. The quarterback may realize that the play called in the huddle won't work against the defense he sees. Or he may realize that another play will work better. So he uses a code word to alert his teammates that he is changing the play, then shouts the new signals.

Though the word "audible" means that a sound can be heard, quarterbacks can also use hand signals to change a play. The point of all this changing is to confuse the defense or to react to a defensive formation. Well-chosen audibles can become game-changing plays.

■ *Peyton Manning calls an audible before the snap.*

■ *Hard-hitting Tommy Nobis (60) smacked in the 1960s.*

Atlanta Falcons

The Atlanta Falcons joined the NFL as an expansion team in 1966. Though the club has yet to win a league championship, it overcame a rocky beginning to field several successful teams in recent years.

Atlanta plays in the South Division of the National Football Conference (NFC). The Falcons joined the Carolina Panthers, the New Orleans Saints, and the Tampa Bay Buccaneers in the newly formed NFC South when the NFL realigned into eight divisions of four teams each in 2002. Before that, the Falcons had played in the NFL Eastern Conference (1966), the NFL Coastal Division (1967–69), and the NFC West (1970–2001).

The Falcons came into being when the NFL moved up its expansion timetable in the late 1960s after discovering that the rival AFL also had its eye on the Georgia capital. Atlanta won just three games in its first season, one in its second, and two in its third, and did not reach the playoffs until 1978. But those early Falcons' teams did produce one of the league's top players in linebacker Tommy Nobis. "Mr. Falcon," as Nobis soon came to be called, was the top overall pick in the 1966 NFL Draft and played 11 seasons for the club.

In 1975, the Falcons selected quarterback Steve Bartkowski with the top overall pick in the draft. Three years later, Bartkowski led Atlanta to a wild-card playoff berth. In 1980, the team won the NFC West for the first time.

By the time he left the Falcons following the 1985 season, Bartkowski had passed for more yards (23,468) and more touchdowns (154) than anyone else in club history.

Other top Falcons players included kick returner Billy "White Shoes" Johnson, running back Gerald Riggs, cornerback Deion Sanders, and linebacker Jessie Tuggle. But playoff seasons were uncommon. The club won only one playoff game between 1979 and 1997.

Atlanta's best season came after Dan Reeves was hired as head coach in 1997. In Reeves' second season, the Falcons were the NFL's surprise team. They won 14 of 16 regular-season games in 1998 behind the passing of quarterback Chris Chandler (25 touchdowns) and the running of Jamal Anderson (1,846 rushing yards). Atlanta reached its first Super Bowl in club history. Only an inspired performance by Broncos quarterback John Elway, who was playing his last game before retiring, kept Atlanta from winning the title.

Reeves brought the Falcons back to the playoffs once more (in 2002), but he was let go late in the 2003 season. Then the club

■ *Exciting Michael Vick leads Atlanta.*

enjoyed another solid season after hiring defensive specialist Jim Mora as head coach in 2004. Mora helped the club go from worst to first in the NFC South, turning its 5–11 record in 2003 around to 11–5 and a division championship his first season as coach.

Athletic quarterback Michael Vick is the headline performer on the current Falcons. He gives opposing defensive coordinators particular problems because of his combination of a cannon left arm and his great running ability. Running back Warrick Dunn is a veteran presence in the backfield, while Pro Bowl defensive end Patrick Kerney leads the defense.

ATLANTA FALCONS

CONFERENCE: NFC

DIVISION: SOUTH

**TEAM COLORS:
BLACK, RED, SILVER, AND WHITE**

**STADIUM (CAPACITY):
GEORGIA DOME
(71,228)**

**ALL-TIME RECORD:
258–374–6**

**NFL CHAMPIONSHIPS
(MOST RECENT):
NONE**

Backfield

Usually the term refers to the area of the field in which the quarterback and running backs line up before the snap. But it also can be a collective term for those players. Similarly, the cornerbacks and safeties on the other side of ball collectively can be called the "defensive backfield."

Bailey, Champ

Perhaps the best coverage cornerback in the NFL, Bailey joined the Denver Broncos in 2004 after playing his first five seasons (1999–2003) with the Washington Redskins.

The 6-foot, 192-pound Bailey, who

■ *Champ Bailey is a shut-down cornerback.*

starred on offense, defense, and special teams in college at Georgia, was the seventh overall pick of the 1999 draft. By his second pro season, he was a starting cornerback in the Pro Bowl.

The Broncos thought so highly of him that in 2004 they sent Clinton Portis, a running back who had gained 1,591 yards the previous season, to Washington to acquire Bailey and a draft choice. Bailey didn't disappoint his new team, making the Pro Bowl each of his first three seasons in Denver. That included 2006, when he intercepted a career-best 10 passes.

Bailey's given first name is Roland, but he was nicknamed "Champ" by his mother when he was a youngster.

Baltimore Ravens

Please see pages 24-25.

Bank of America Stadium

The home of the NFL's Carolina Panthers since the franchise's second year in 1996. The expansion Panthers played their home games at Clemson, South Carolina, in their inaugural season in 1995 while waiting for their new stadium to be built. Bank of America Stadium is located in Charlotte, North Carolina. It was originally called Ericsson Stadium until Bank of America purchased the naming rights in 2004. The natural-grass stadium can hold 73,298 fans.

Baugh, Sammy

One of the first of the great T-formation quarterbacks, Sammy Baugh helped revolutionize pro football with his forward passing in the 1930s and 1940s. He played 16 seasons for the Washington Redskins beginning in 1937 and was a charter member of the Pro Football Hall of Fame in 1963.

Baugh entered the NFL with the nickname "Slingin' Sammy," earned on the baseball diamond at Texas Christian University, but it worked in football, too!

Baugh originally was kind of a running back in the days when football primarily was "three yards and a cloud of dust" (or lots of short runs). But he quickly showed he could pass very well, too. The story goes that when he first arrived in Washington, coach Ray Flaherty asked him to hit a Redskins' receiver "in the eye"—a common expression. "Sure, Coach," Baugh drawled. "Which eye?" When the passing-heavy T-formation came in, Baugh switched to quarterback in 1944.

Baugh was an excellent all-around athlete, too. In a time when players played both offense and defense, he excelled as a defensive back. He was also a top punter who averaged 51.3 yards per kick in 1940, a record that still stands. In 1943, he led the NFL in offensive (passing), defensive (interceptions), and special-teams (punting) categories.

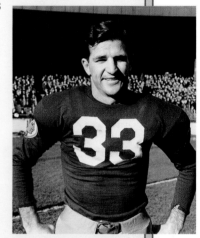

■ QB "Slingin'"
Sammy Baugh

Barber, Tiki and Ronde

Tiki Barber and Ronde Barber are identical twin brothers who starred on for the New York Giants and Tampa Bay Buccaneers. Tiki was a Pro Bowl running back for New York; Ronde is a Pro Bowl cornerback for Tampa Bay.

Both players stand 5 feet 10 inches (Tiki is listed at 200 pounds, while Ronde is 184) and were drafted out of Virginia in 1997. Tiki was chosen by the Giants in the second round, while Ronde went one round later to the Buccaneers.

Tiki was one of the top rushing and receiving threats in the NFL. His 2,390 yards from scrimmage in 2005 were the second-most in a season in league history. He also broke his own record for the most rushing yards in Giants' history that year (1,860) and is the club's all-time leading rusher (10,449 yards).

Ronde has been a cornerstone of the strong defenses that have been a hallmark

continued on page 26

ing the 1995 season. The Browns' team colors, logos, and history all stayed in Cleveland (and were picked up by the new Cleveland Browns in 1999), while the players and administrators officially began as a new team in 1996. Baltimore's nickname came from Edgar Allan Poe's famous poem, "The Raven." Though not a native of Baltimore, Poe spent much of his adult life in the city.

After several mediocre years in Baltimore, the Ravens stood at 5 wins and 4 losses midway through the 2000 season. But they would not lose again that year, winning their final seven regular-season games to earn a wild-card playoff berth.

To get to the postseason, the Ravens relied on a stifling defense that permitted their opponents only 165 points during the regular season. No other NFL team had allowed fewer points since the league went to a 16-game schedule in 1978. Middle linebacker Ray Lewis, a first-round draft pick in 1996, emerged as the most dominant defensive

Baltimore Ravens

The Ravens have been in existence since 1996. They have traditionally featured a strong defense, including a record-setting unit in 2000 that carried them to their lone Super Bowl championship.

The Ravens were born when the Cleveland Browns moved to Baltimore follow-

force in the NFL. He was named the league's defensive player of the year for 2000 by the Associated Press. Lewis and fellow Ravens' defenders Sam Adams, a defensive tackle, and Rod Woodson, a safety, were named as starters for the AFC squad in the Pro Bowl that season.

In the 2000 playoffs, the Ravens rode their defense to easy victories over Denver (21–3), Tennessee (24–10), and Oakland (16–3) to win the AFC championship. Baltimore then crushed the New York Giants 34–7 to win Super Bowl XXXV in Tampa, Florida. The Ravens' defense was dominant again, permitting the Giants only 152 yards while forcing 5 turnovers. New York's lone points came on a kickoff return for a touchdown, and Lewis was named the game's MVP.

Since then, the Ravens have continued to field strong defenses that ranked among the NFL's top six five times in six seasons from 2001 to 2006. But their offense has not been able to keep pace, often ranking among the league's poorest teams. Even in the championship season of 2000, Baltimore did not score a touchdown for 21 quarters,

■ *LB Ray Lewis is a powerhouse defender.*

one of the longest such streaks in modern NFL history.

Baltimore's most significant offensive accomplishment came in 2003, when workhorse running back Jamal Lewis (no relation to Ray Lewis) gained a club-record 2,066 yards on the ground. He became just the fifth NFL player to run for 2,000 yards in a season, and his season total is the second best in league history behind only Eric Dickerson's 2,105 yards for the Rams in 1984. Even still, with the league's poorest passing offense in 2003, the Ravens reached the playoffs that year. In 2006, they had a 13-3 record and another playoff berth.

BALTIMORE RAVENS

CONFERENCE: **AFC**

DIVISION: **NORTH**

TEAM COLORS: **BLACK, PURPLE, AND METALLIC GOLD**

STADIUM (CAPACITY): **M&T BANK STADIUM (69,084)**

ALL-TIME RECORD (THROUGH 2006): **83–83–1**

NFL CHAMPIONSHIPS (MOST RECENT): **1 (2000)**

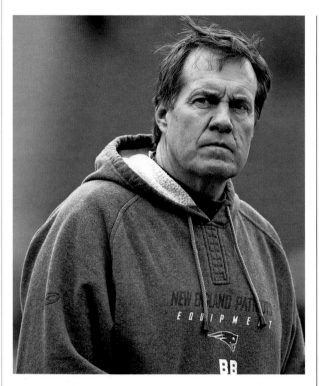

■ *Bill Belichick has won three Super Bowls.*

in Tampa Bay since becoming a full-time starter in 1998. He made the Pro Bowl for the first time in the 2001 season. In 2005, he became the first cornerback in NFL history to amass at least 20 career interceptions and 20 career sacks.

In addition to their on-field accomplishments, the twins are budding media stars who have hosted their own show on Sirius satellite radio. In 2004, they penned their first illustrated children's book, called *By My Brother's Side.*

Bednarik, Chuck

Former Philadelphia Eagles star Chuck Bednarik was known as the "Last of the 60-Minute Men." When Bednarik entered the NFL in 1949, players often still lined up on both sides of the ball. But by the time he retired in 1962, most players stayed on either offense or defense. Bednarik, however, continued to excel as a center on offense and a linebacker on defense.

Bednarik's crowning moment came in the 1960 NFL Championship Game against Green Bay. At 35 years old, he had helped the Eagles reach the title match by playing both ways in a series of games leading up to it. Then he played more than 50 of the game's 60 minutes against the Packers. On the final play of the game, he tackled Green Bay running back Jim Taylor inside Philadelphia's 10-yard line to preserve the Eagles' 17–13 victory. It was the only time that legendary Packers coach Vince Lombardi lost a postseason game.

In 1967, Bednarik was inducted into the Pro Football Hall of Fame.

Belichick, Bill

The architect of the Patriots' immense success in the early 2000s, Bill Belichick is the only head coach ever to lead his team to three Super Bowl victories in a four-year span. His teams are known for their discipline and selfless team play.

A protégé of long-time NFL head coach Bill Parcells, Belichick was the defensive coordinator under Parcells for the Giants Super Bowl championship teams in 1986 and 1990. He was only 38 years when the

Bell, Bert

Pro football was another game—a smaller game—when Bert Bell was its commissioner from 1946-1959. The NFL dominates American sports today. It didn't then.

There were only 10 NFL teams in Bell's first four years as commissioner, and 12 most of the time in his last 10 years. There are 32 teams today.

In Bell's day, each team sent one or two people to a league meeting. And they often met in Bert Bell's hotel room. Legend had it that the beloved commissioner often conducted the meetings dressed in nothing but boxer shorts and an undershirt. (Imagine Paul Tagliabue or Roger Goodell running an NFL meeting in their underwear!)

Bell always was a strong leader and a creative thinker. Founder and co-owner of the Philadelphia Eagles in 1933, Bell had a big idea in 1936 that brought competitive balance to the game. He suggested the NFL begin a draft—teams would select college players, with the poorest records going first.

Elected commissioner to succeed Elmer Layden in 1946, Bell faced two immediate problems—a potential "point fixing" crisis and a rival new league, the All-America Football Conference (AAFC).

On the eve of the 1946 NFL Championship Game between the Chicago Bears and the New York Giants, Bell learned that two Giants' stars—quarterback Frank Filchock and halfback Merle Hapes—had been approached by gamblers about "fixing" the point spread in the game in exchange for money.

Both men had said no to the illegal offer but they had not reported it. Hapes was suspended. Filchock was allowed to play, but was suspended later. These actions marked the start of tough NFL anti-gambling rules.

Bell helped the NFL win the rivalry with the AAFC. In 1950, the AAFC folded and three of its teams—Cleveland, San Francisco, and Baltimore—were added to the NFL.

On October 11, 1959, Bell was in Philadelphia's Shibe Park to watch the Eagles play the Steelers. With two minutes left to play, he suffered a massive heart and died at 64.—J.W.

■ *Bell (right) with Steelers owner Art Rooney*

Cleveland Browns hired him as their head coach in 1991.

Belichick rebuilt the Browns, turning a 3–13 squad that he inherited into an 11–5 team that made the playoffs in 1994. He later rejoined Parcells as an assistant with the New York Jets, then was hired in 2000 to lead the Patriots.

In just his second season in New England, Belichick guided the Patriots to their first Super Bowl championship. They added back-to-back titles in 2003 and 2004. Along the way, New England set an NFL record by winning 18 consecutive regular-season games to end the 2003 season and start 2004. The Patriots' 34 total victories those two years (including postseason) marked the most by any team in a two-year period in NFL history.

Berry, Raymond

Raymond Berry was a Pro Football Hall of Fame wide receiver for the Baltimore Colts from 1955 to 1967. At the time of his retirement, he held the NFL's all-time record with 631 career receptions.

Bettis, Jerome

Jerome Bettis was known as "The Bus" for the way that he barreled through opposing defenses for 13 years.

The Rams made the burly 5-foot 11-inch, 255-pound running back the 10th overall pick in 1993. Despite a couple of 1,000-yard seasons, the club shipped him to Pittsburgh in 1996. He fit right in with the run-oriented Steelers, and had six consecutive years of more than 1,000 yards on the ground. Even late in his career, when he no longer was an every-down back, he remained a valuable force near the goal line, and continued to help the Steelers by moving the chains on third-down and short-yardage situations. At age 32 in 2004, he ran for 13 touchdowns.

■ *Here comes the Bus on a roll.*

In 2005, Bettis capped his career by helping the Pittsburgh Steelers win Super Bowl XL. The title game, a 21–10 victory over Seattle, came in his hometown of Detroit, Michigan.

Bettis ranks fifth on the NFL's all-time rushing list with 13,662 career yards. The Bus will be eligible for his bid drive into the Pro Football Hall of Fame beginning in 2011.

Not very big or fast, Berry was blessed with remarkable determination and sure hands—and had a future Pro Football Hall of Fame quarterback in John Unitas throwing the ball to him.

Berry and Unitas formed one of the greatest passing tandems in NFL history. Their 63 touchdown connections were the most ever at the time, and still rank fifth on the NFL's all-time list nearly 40 years later. Berry and Unitas also teamed on several key passes in the Colts' famous 23–17 victory over the New York Giants in overtime in the 1958 NFL Championship Game.

Berry was a six-time Pro Bowl player who later went on to coach the New England Patriots to Super Bowl XX in the 1985 season. He was inducted into the Pro Football Hall of Fame in 1973.

Biletnikoff, Fred

On the rollicking Oakland Raiders' teams of the 1960s and 1970s, Fred Biletnikoff was a steady, if unspectacular, force at wide receiver for 14 seasons beginning in 1965.

A precise route runner with sure hands, Biletnikoff caught 589 passes in his career, the most in club history at the time of his retirement in 1978. In typical understated fashion, Biletnikoff was the most valuable player of the Raiders' 32-14 rout of the Minnesota Vikings in Super Bowl XI to cap the 1976 season. He caught a modest

Blanda, George

George Blanda was an iron man who played a record 26 NFL seasons and was the first player in league history to score more than 2,000 points. But he is also remembered for a remarkable five-game stretch in 1970 during which he led the Raiders to five wins or ties—at age 43!

Blanda was a quarterback and kicker for the Bears and Colts before coming out of retirement in 1960 to play for the Houston Oilers of the new AFL. Seven years later, he joined the Raiders.

He was a backup quarterback for Oakland,

■ *No one played more NFL seasons than George Blanda.*

but was called on to replace injured Daryle Lamonica in a game against Pittsburgh. With field goals and touchdown passes, he helped them reel off five wins or ties. Blanda played five more seasons after that, mostly at kicker, before retiring at age 48 following the 1975 season. He went into the Hall of Fame in 1981.

4 passes for 79 yards, with no touchdowns. But 3 of his receptions directly preceded short Raiders' scoring runs or passes.

Blitz

A pass rush in which designated linebackers or defensive backs join the usual down linemen in rushing the quarterback. Defensive teams thus sacrifice pass coverage for increased pressure on the quarterback.

Block

Primarily, when an offensive player legally obstructs a defensive player from reaching the ball carrier. It also can refer to

the action of a defensive player who knocks down a punt, field goal, or extra-point.

Blount, Mel

One of the several future Pro Football Hall of Fame members on the Steelers' defense of the 1970s, Mel Blount blanketed opposing wide receivers from his cornerback position in a 14-year career that ended in 1983.

At 6 feet 3 inches, 205 pounds, and blessed with wide-receiver speed, Blount was a match for any opposing pass catcher. His pass coverage helped the "Steel Curtain's" defensive line pressure the quarterback.

Blount's best season came in 1975, when he set a club record by intercepting 11 passes for the Steelers' Super Bowl champions and was named the NFL's defensive player of the year. He was inducted into the Pro Football Hall of Fame in 1989.

Boldin, Anquan

Anquan Boldin is a prolific young wide receiver who first burst onto the NFL scene with a record-setting rookie season for the Arizona Cardinals in 2003.

The 6-1, 223-pound Bold-

■ *No. 77 in this photo is blocking his opponent in black.*

in was a second-round draft pick out of Florida State that year. Against Detroit on Kickoff Weekend, he amassed 217 receiving yards—the most ever by an NFL player in his first game. By season's end, Boldin had caught more passes (101) than any other rookie in league history.

After a knee injury slowed him in 2004, he bounced back to catch 102 passes the next season. He is the only player ever to surpass 100 catches two times in his first three years in the NFL.

Bomb

A slang term for a long pass. It's one of several war-related terms ("attack" and "in the trenches" are other examples) that have made their way into football lingo.

Box

An unofficial designation for the imaginary area near the line of scrimmage in which most defenders position themselves. Typically, seven defensive players line up in the box (either four linemen and three linebackers or three linemen and four linebackers). When a defensive team brings an eighth man into the box, it usually is trying to stop the run.

Bradshaw, Terry

Terry Bradshaw, who was inducted into the Pro Football Hall of Fame in 1989, quarterbacked the Pittsburgh Steelers

■ *Bradshaw was known for his strong arm.*

to four Super Bowl victories in the 1970s.

Bradshaw was the number-one overall pick in the 1970 draft out of Louisiana Tech. Early in his pro career, he was a quarterback whose primary responsibility was to hand off the ball on the Steelers' run-oriented, defense-dominated teams that won back-to-back Super Bowls in the 1974 and 1975 seasons.

But he soon changed into a feared passer who led Pittsburgh to Super Bowl victories in 1978 and 1979 with his rocket arm. Indeed, he was the most valuable player of the club's wins over Dallas in game XIII (he passed for 318 yards and 4 touchdowns in a 35-31 victory) and the Los Angeles Rams in game XIV (309 yards and 2 touchdowns in a 31-19 win).

Bradshaw retired from his playing career following the 1983 season holding

31

Brady, Tom

A superb leader, Tom Brady quarterbacked the New England Patriots to three Super Bowl championships in the early 2000s. He is one of only four NFL quarterbacks to start in the Super Bowl for three winning teams.

Despite having led the University of Michigan to a 10-win season in 1999, Brady largely was overlooked in the 2000 NFL Draft because of perceived physical limitations. The Patriots did not select him until the sixth round, the 199th player chosen.

Brady made the team as a rookie in 2000, and when New England starting quarterback Drew Bledsoe was injured early in the 2001 season, Tom stepped into the lineup—and he's been there ever since.

After leading the Patriots to the playoffs in 2001, Brady began building his reputation as a big-game winner by rallying New England from behind to beat the Raiders in a dramatic AFC Divisional Playoff Game.

■ *The Patriots' "Tom Terrific."*

Several weeks later, against the heavily favored St. Louis Rams in Super Bowl XXXVI, Brady calmly led his team to the winning field goal as time ran out. Brady was named the most valuable player of that game, as well as of the Patriots' 32-29 victory over the Carolina Panthers two seasons later in Super Bowl XXXVIII. The next year, he guided New England to a 24–21 victory over Philadelphia in Super Bowl XXXIX.

club records of 27,989 passing yards and 212 touchdown passes. He is still familiar to football fans as a long-time network studio analyst for NFL games on television.

Brees, Drew

Quarterback Drew Brees helped the San Diego Chargers achieve surprising success in 2004 and 2005. He joined with LaDainian Tomlinson to give the "Bolts" a powerful offensive punch. However, following the 2005 season, the team turned to young passer Philip Rivers. Brees signed a six-year, $60-million contract to lead the New Orleans Saints.

In his new home, Brees flourished. The Saints made the playoffs for the first time in six years. Brees was among league passing leaders and set an all-time record by passing for more than 1,900 total yards over five consecutive games. He led the Saints to their first-ever appearance in the NFC Championship Game.

Brooks, Derrick

Derrick Brooks is a big-play linebacker who has starred for the Tampa Bay Buccaneers' defense ever since he was drafted out of Florida State in the first round in 1995.

Brooks, who stands 6 feet and weighs 235 pounds, began a string of nine consecutive Pro Bowl appearances in the 1997 season. His best year came in 2002, when the Buccaneers' dominating defense carried the club to a Super Bowl championship. Brooks scored 4 touchdowns that season, returning 3 interceptions (a record for an NFL linebacker) and a fumble for scores. He was named the NFL's defensive player of the year.

Off the field, Brooks is a respected member of the community who shared the NFL's Walter Payton Man of the Year Award for 2000 and who serves on Florida State's Board of Trustees.

Brown, Roosevelt

Perhaps the biggest draft-day sleeper in history, tackle Roosevelt Brown was just a 27th-round selection out of Morgan State in 1953 who went on to become one of the greatest offensive linemen in NFL history.

Not many folks knew about Brown when he walked into his first New York Giants' training camp as a 20-year-old his rookie season. But he earned a starting spot on the club's offensive line his first year, and he remained in the lineup for 13 seasons until retiring in 1965.

Equally good at run blocking or protecting the passer, Brown was an all-league

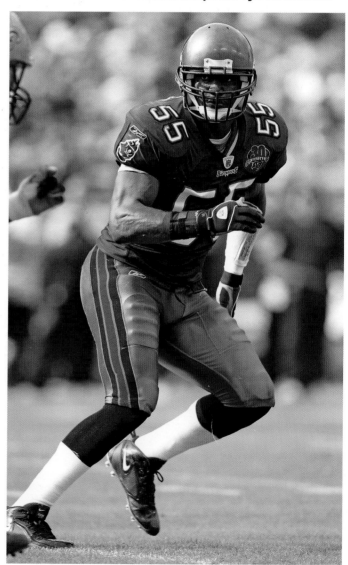

■ *Linebacker Derrick Brooks keeps his eye on the ball.*

choice for eight consecutive seasons beginning in 1956. He helped the Giants reach the NFL Championship Game six times in his career, highlighted by a title win in 1956. In 1975, Brown was inducted into the Pro Football Hall of Fame.

Brown, Tim

A dynamic wide receiver whose pass-catching skills were rivaled only by his kick-return abilities, former Raiders star Tim Brown is one of only four players in NFL history to amass more than 1,000

continued on page 38

Brown, Jim

An All-America running back at Syracuse, Jim Brown joined the Cleveland Browns as a first-round draft pick in 1957 and hit the ground running.

Brown's nine seasons included just 118 regular-season games. Brown's average per game was a record 104.3 rushing yards. To get to his then-record 12,312 career yards—a mark that stood until Walter Payton eclipsed it two decades later—Brown averaged a record 5.2 yards a carry. In nine years, Brown never missed a game.

He was Rookie of the Year in 1957, when he led the league with what would be his lowest single-season total, 942 yards. He led the NFL in seven of the

■ *Big Jim Brown: football's best?*

next eight seasons, with totals ranging from 1,257 yards in 12 games in 1960 to 1,863 yards in 14 games in 1963.

After the 1962 season, Brown led a rebellion against his head coach, Paul Brown. The running back felt he wasn't being used properly (in '62, he had his lowest average per carry, 4.3). He went to new owner Art Modell, who replaced Paul Brown with Blanton Collier. Under Collier, Brown responded with three great years, averaging more than 1,600 yards a season and 5.6 yards a carry. Cleveland won the 1964 NFL championship over Baltimore 27-0, and almost repeated in 1965, when Brown was NFL MVP.

He was making a movie, The Dirty Dozen, in the summer of 1966 and, because of a delay in the shooting schedule, was late for Browns' training camp. When Modell announced that Brown would be fined for every day of camp he missed, Brown, 30, called a press conference to announce that he was quitting the game. He never played again.

In 1999, NFL Films named Jim Brown "NFL Player of the Millennium." — J. W.

Brown, Paul

Before Paul Brown, football coaching was mostly a part-time job. Brown changed all that in a lifetime spent in Ohio. He grew up in Massillon, Ohio, where he was an undersized high school and college quarterback (for Miami of Ohio).

Brown was an Ohio coaching success at every level. At 24, Brown became the head coach at Massillon High; his teams were unbeaten in 1938, 1939, and 1940. He moved to Ohio State, where he turned a Buckeyes' team that had lost 40-0 to Michigan to end the previous season into a Big Ten co-champion. Then, during World War II, Brown coached a military team at Great Lakes Naval Training Center to a 15-2 record.

When the war ended, Brown accepted another challenge in 1946: to lead the Cleveland Browns' team in the new All-America Football Conference. Brown signed a player he had seen while at Great Lakes, quarterback Otto Graham. Led by those two men, Cleveland dominated the league for

■ *Brown only coached in Ohio, but he had national impact.*

four years. Brown's teams were so strong they helped drive the AAFC out of business and the Browns into the NFL.

In its first game against an NFL team in 1950, Cleveland defeated the defending NFL-champion Eagles 35–10. The Browns went on to win the 1950 NFL title.

Brown and Graham teamed up for five more years. They reached the NFL Championship Game five times, winning two of them (1954 and 1955). Graham retired before the 1956 season, but the great running back Jim Brown was drafted in 1957, and the team was back in the title game again that year. A new Browns' owner, Art Modell, fired Brown after the 1962 season.

A few years later, Brown was back in football in—where else?—Ohio. At age 60, he became the owner-coach of the newly formed Cincinnati Bengals, a dual role he held for eight years. Then, at 68, he retired after the 1975 season.

Few coaches have been as successful for as long as Paul Brown, a true NFL legend. He was inducted into the Pro Football Hall of Fame in 1967. –J. W.

Buffalo Bills

One of the eight charter members of the American Football League (AFL) in 1960, the Bills' history has been filled with lots of highs and lows. They have yet to reach the ultimate high, though: winning a Super Bowl.

■ *Kelly was a creative Bills' leader.*

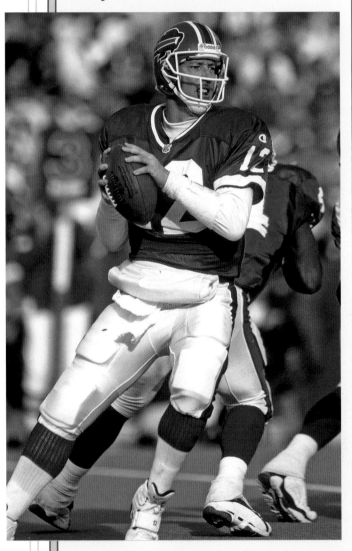

Ralph Wilson was a minority stockholder of the NFL's Detroit Lions in the late 1950s. But he was anxious to field a team of his own and was granted a franchise in the newly formed AFL. Wilson originally wanted to place his team in Miami. When he couldn't arrange to play home games in that city's Orange Bowl, he opted for Buffalo instead.

The Bills turned out to be one of the AFL's most successful franchises, both on the field and at the gate. On the field, they reached the postseason for four consecutive years beginning in 1963. Behind future United States Congressman Jack Kemp at quarterback, future Pro Football Hall of Fame guard Billy Shaw anchoring the offensive line, and the AFL's best defense, Buffalo won back-to-back league titles in 1964 and 1965. At the gate, the club was supported by some of the league's most enthusiastic fans. Buffalo led the AFL in home attendance three times in the league's 10-year existence.

Things did not go as well on the field after a loss to Kansas City in the 1966 AFL Championship Game kept the Bills from reaching the first Super Bowl. In the early 1970s, Buffalo featured a superstar in running back O.J. Simpson, who became the first NFL player to run for more than 2,000 yards in a season in 1973, but the Bills reached the playoffs just three times from 1967 to 1987.

Then in 1988, rookie running back Thurman Thomas joined quarterback Jim Kelly and wide receiver Andre Reed to give the Bills a powerful offense. Head coach Marv Levy used a no-huddle attack to keep the pressure on opposing defenses. The offense helped carry the Bills to a 12-4 record and the AFC East title.

That was a sign of things to come. The Bills won five more division titles in the next seven seasons, including 1990, when they won the AFC championship and reached the Super Bowl for the first time. In one of the most exciting Super Bowls ever, they narrowly lost to the New York Giants 20–19 in game XXV when Scott Norwood's 47-yard field goal try in the final seconds sailed wide.

It was the first of several heartbreaks for Bills' fans. Buffalo reached the Super Bowl each of the next three years, only to fall short in the title game each time. In 1992, the Bills even staged the greatest comeback in NFL history in the wild-card playoffs, beating Houston 41-38 in overtime after trailing 35-3 in the third quarter, but they eventually were routed by the Cowboys in Super Bowl XXVII.

So on one hand, no other NFL team has played in four consecutive Super Bowls (and only the 1971–73 Miami Dolphins have played in as many as three). On the other hand, the four straight Super Bowl losses kept those Bills' teams from being recognized among football's all-time greats.

Since earning wild-card playoff berths in 1998 and 1999 but being ousted in the first round each of those years, the Bills have not returned to the postseason. Levy, who coached the Bills from 1986 to 1997, was brought back as general manager in 2006 to help restore the club's fortunes. He immediately began building around running back Willis McGahee, a first-round draft choice who ran for more than 1,000 yards in two of his first three seasons (2004–2006), speedy receiver Lee Evans, and quarterback J.P. Losman.

■ *Speedy Willis McGahee powers the Bills' offense.*

BUFFALO BILLS

CONFERENCE: AFC

DIVISION: EAST

TEAM COLORS: DARK NAVY, RED, ROYAL, AND NICKEL

STADIUM (CAPACITY): RALPH WILSON STADIUM (73,967)

ALL-TIME RECORD: 348–381–8

NFL CHAMPIONSHIPS (MOST RECENT): 2* (1965)

* includes AFL

receptions in his career (along with Jerry Rice, Cris Carter, and Marvin Harrison). The 1987 Heisman Trophy winner at Notre Dame, Brown was the sixth overall selection in the following spring's NFL draft. He made an immediate impact, leading the league in kickoff returns in 1988 and setting a league rookie record with 2,317 combined net yards (rushing, receiving, and returns). In later years, Brown also topped the league in punt returns (1994) and in receptions (1997).

Brown played 16 seasons for the Raiders, then retired after one season in Tampa Bay in 2004. He can be voted into the Pro Football Hall of Fame in 2010.

Bruce, Isaac

The Rams' long tradition of great pass receivers includes the likes of Pro Football Hall of Famers such as Tom Fears and Elroy "Crazylegs" Hirsch. But no one in the club's storied history caught as many career passes as Isaac Bruce.

A second-round draft choice out of Memphis State in 1994, Bruce blossomed into a star by his second NFL season, when he set Rams' records with 119 receptions for 1,781 yards. He played a key role on St. Louis' "Greatest Show on Turf" offenses of the late 1990s and early 2000s, stringing together four consecutive 1,000-yard receiving seasons starting with the club's Super Bowl-winning season in 1999.

Bruce closed the 2006 season holding franchise marks for career receptions (887), receiving yards (13,376), and touchdown catches (80).

Buchanan, Buck

Junious "Buck" Buchanan of the Kansas City Chiefs' was one of the dominant defensive tackles of his era. At 6 feet 7 inches, Buchanan had the size to bat down opposing quarterback's throws. At 270 pounds, he had the strength to bully his way past offensive lineman. And with 10.2 speed in the 100-yard dash, he had the quick-

■ *Isaac Bruce is among the NFL"s all-time best.*

Butkus, Dick

The perfect example of the modern middle linebacker, Dick Butkus was a ferocious defender for the Chicago Bears for nine seasons in the mid-1960s to early 1970s. A punishing hitter capable of stopping opposing ball carriers in their tracks, Butkus also had the speed and agility to cover receivers or to rush the quarterback.

The second first-round draft choice of the Bears in 1965 (the first was running back Gale Sayers, another future Pro Football Hall of Famer), Butkus was a starter just about from the day he walked into his first training camp that year. He went on to earn a Pro Bowl selection his rookie year, and his speed,

■ Feared defender Dick Butkus

intensity, and desire earned him return trips to the NFL's annual all-star game each of the next seven seasons.

About the only thing that could stop Butkus was injury, and that was what ended his career after nine seasons. He never bounced fully back from a knee injury suffered in the 1970 season. Despite two more Pro Bowl years after that, he was forced to retire following the 1973 season.

In 1979, he was inducted into the Pro Football Hall of Fame.

ness to chase down opposing ball carriers all over the field. Buchanan played in eight AFL All-Star Games or NFL Pro Bowls in his 13-year career. In 1990, he was inducted into the Pro Football Hall of Fame.

Buffalo Bills

Please see pages 36-37.

Bump-and-run

A defensive technique in which a player (usually a cornerback) lines up directly in front of a wide receiver, "bumps" him when he comes off the line of scrimmage, then turns and "runs" with him in one-on-one coverage. Bumping is only allowed within five yards of the line of scrimmage.

Bush, Reggie

After helping USC win two national championships and earning the Heisman Trophy, Reggie Bush joined the New Orleans Saints in 2006 and became a solid performer. New Orleans was looking for an impact player in the season they returned to the city after 2005's Hurricane Katrina. Bush was among rookie leaders in rushing and touchdowns, while becoming a symbol of the team in the community.

Canadian Football League

The Canadian Football League (CFL), founded in 1958, has eight teams, all located in Canada. The CFL had some teams in the U.S. in the 1990s.

Like American football, Canadian football has its roots in rugby, but various rules differences have evolved over the years. The Canadian field is longer (by 10 yards) and wider (by nearly 12 yards), and the end zones are deeper (by 10 yards each). Teams in Canada play with 12 players on each side (instead of 11), they have only three downs (instead of four) to make the 10 yards for a first down. Scoring includes "singles." Kicks that go through the end zone or are not returned out of the end zone result in one point for the kicking team.

Campbell, Earl

Earl Campbell was a bruising running back who combined power and speed like few other players in NFL history. He played eight seasons in the NFL from 1978 to 1985, mostly for the Houston Oilers, and was inducted into the Pro Football Hall of Fame in his first year of eligibility in 1991.

In 1978, the Oilers traded four draft picks (including a first-rounder and a second-rounder) and star tight end Jimmie Giles for the right to select Campbell with the top overall choice. The Heisman Trophy winner from Texas immediately made that look like a good deal by rushing for 1,450 yards in his rookie season and earning league MVP honors. He went on to win three consecutive NFL rushing titles, and by the time he finished his career with one-and-a-half seasons in New Orleans, he had rushed for 9,407 yards in only 115 games.

Campbell's most famous game came on a Monday night against Miami in his rookie season. He bulled his way for 199 yards in a 35–30 victory, including an 81-yard touchdown burst for the clinching touchdown late in the fourth quarter.

Earl Campbell was very hard to stop.

Some NFL stars, such as former quarterbacks Warren Moon and Joe Theismann and kicker Mike Vanderjagt, got their starts in the CFL.

Canton Bulldogs

The Canton Bulldogs were perhaps the most successful, and certainly the best known, of the pro football teams in the Midwest before the formation of the NFL in 1920. Then they enjoyed a couple of very successful years in the new league before breaking up and going out of business following the 1926 season.

The Bulldogs, who featured legendary Olympian Jim Thorpe, were original members of the NFL (then called the American Professional Football Association) in 1920. The Bulldogs were crowned NFL champions when they went undefeated in both 1922 (10–0–2) and 1923 (11–0–1). The team was sold the next year, though, and many of its best players played for the newly named Cleveland Bulldogs, who won the 1924 league title.

Canton fielded a team in 1925, but folded for good after two unsuccessful years. The Ohio town got a permanent place in NFL history when the Pro Football Hall of Fame opened there in 1963.

Carolina Panthers

Please see pages 42-43.

■ *Casper scores in Super Bowl XI.*

Carr, Joe

Please see page 44.

Casper, Dave

A Pro Football Hall of Fame tight end who was as good a pass catcher as he was a blocker, Dave Casper played 11 NFL seasons (1974–1984) for the Raiders, Oilers, and Vikings.

A second-round draft pick by Oakland in 1974, Casper helped the Raiders win Super Bowl XI in 1976 by catching 53

continued on page 45

■ *Big Julius Peppers is a pass-rushing threat.*

Carolina Panthers

The Carolina Panthers joined the NFL as an expansion franchise in 1995. They reached the conference championship game in only their second season of existence; before their first decade was out, they were in the Super Bowl.

It was quickly apparent that first-time head coach Dom Capers' Panthers were no ordinary expansion team. Before they entered the league along with the Jacksonville Jaguars, no other expansion team had won more than four games in a season. But Carolina won seven times in its first year, including a shocking 13–7 upset of the 49ers—the team that had won Super Bowl XXIX in the 1994 season—in a game at San Francisco. It was the first time that an expansion team ever had beaten a reigning Super Bowl champion.

The Panthers soon proved that the upset was no fluke, however. The next year, Carolina beat the 49ers twice. And when the Panthers beat Pittsburgh 18–14 on the final week of the 1996 season, the two wins over San Francisco gave them the tiebreaker edge and earned them their first division title with a 12–4 record.

Two weeks later, Carolina hosted the first postseason game in its brief history. The Panthers thrilled the home crowd with a 26–17 victory over the Dallas Cowboys, a franchise that already had won three Super Bowls in the decade. Though Carolina's own Super Bowl hopes were dashed by a loss at Green Bay in the NFC Championship Game, the Panthers had served notice to the rest of the league that they were a force to be reckoned with.

Carolina sent eight players to the Pro Bowl in its second season, including quarterback Kerry Collins tight end Wesley Walls, and linebackers Sam Mills, Kevin Greene, and Lamar Lathon. The special teams featured kicker John Kasay, who set an NFL record by kicking 37 field goals, and dynamic kick returner Michael Bates.

It took several seasons (and a couple of coaching changes) for Carolina to build on its early success, but things all came together in 2003, under coach John Fox, for the club's first Super Bowl trip.

After winning four of its last five games in 2002, Carolina opened the 2003 season with five consecutive victories and cruised to the NFC South title with an 11–5 record. The Panthers beat Dallas again at home in the playoffs before taking to the road to register upsets of the St. Louis Rams and the Philadelphia Eagles. The latter, a 14–3 victory in which Fox's defense shut down the Eagles' explosive offense, sent Carolina to Super Bowl XXXVIII against New England.

CAROLINA PANTHERS

CONFERENCE: NFC

DIVISION: SOUTH

TEAM COLORS:
BLACK, PANTHER BLUE, AND SILVER

STADIUM (CAPACITY):
BANK OF AMERICA STADIUM (73,298)

ALL-TIME RECORD:
96–105–0

NFL CHAMPIONSHIPS (MOST RECENT):
NONE

The Patriots, who were in the midst of an historic three Super Bowl victories in a four-season stretch, won an exciting game 32–29 with a field goal in the final seconds. The Panthers were big underdogs in the game, so their performance was impressive. While the Panthers have not been back to the NFL's big game since, they have established themselves as legitimate title contenders under Fox.

The former defensive coordinator of the New York Giants in their NFC championship season of 2000, Fox came to Carolina with a reputation as a defensive mastermind. The Panthers' defense has indeed been successful with players such as all-star defensive end Julius Peppers, but Fox also has built a prolific offense around quarterback Jake Delhomme and wide receiver Steve Smith, who is one of the NFL's most exciting players.

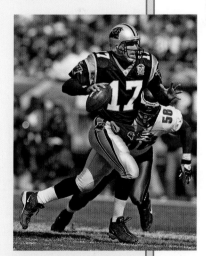

■ *Gutsy Jake Delhomme leads the Carolina offense.*

Carr, Joe

Joe Carr was president of the National Football League for 19 years (the man who ran the NFL then was called "president," not "commissioner"). NFL owners gave Carr the job in 1921 and he kept it until he died of a heart attack in May 1939 at age 59.

Carr was a true pioneer of the game, a man who was there in the Hupmobile showroom on August 20, 1920, when a group formed was eventually called the American Professional Football Association (APFA). Carr was the owner of the Columbus Panhandles.

Two years later, when Carr was president,

■ *Joe Carr (left) with player Danny Fortmann.*

the APFA was renamed the National Football League. For two decades, Joe Carr's name was synonymous with the NFL. He would lead the league longer than all but one of the men who would follow him (Pete Rozelle was commissioner for 29 years, 1960-1989).

Carr took the NFL out of the small towns and into the big cities. He brought the game to the attention of America. He led the NFL to victory over its first competition—Red Grange's American Football League in 1926.

Carr organized the NFL into divisions and introduced the championship game. He banned college undergraduates from the NFL. He produced the first standard player contract. He enforced strict gambling laws. He led the league through its toughest times, the Great Depression days of the 1930s.

And for all he did in the NFL, when the Pro Football Hall of Fame began in 1963, Joe Carr was among the first 17 men to be honored.

But football was only part of Carr's remarkable life. He started a semipro baseball team; he was a sports editor and writer; and he was the American Basketball Association's first president in 1925. Even while serving as NFL president, he was the executive director of the minor-league National Baseball Association.

A "Renaissance man" is someone who has widely varying interests. Joe Carr was a true Renaissance sportsman. But he always said his first love was the NFL. — J. W.

passes, including 10 for touchdowns. The next season, his famous "Ghost to the Post" catch–Casper's nickname was "Ghost," after the children's cartoon character–helped the Raiders beat the Colts in a divisional playoff game.

In all, Casper caught 378 passes in his career and went to five Pro Bowls.

"The Catch"

Dwight Clark's leaping, 6-yard touchdown grab in the final minute of the 1981 NFC Championship Game has become known simply as "The Catch." Clark's reception of a Joe Montana pass lifted the San Francisco 49ers to a 28–27 win over the Dallas Cowboys.

The play capped a 13-play, 89-yard march that began with 4:54 remaining and the 49ers trailing 27–21. On third down from the Cowboys' 6-yard line, Montana rolled right and threw off his back foot under heavy pressure from the Dallas pass rush. His high pass looked as if was heading out of the end zone until the 6-4 Clark snared it with his fingertips.

The Catch is so significant not only because it remains one of the most exciting plays in NFL history, but also because it marked the beginning of a dynasty in San

■ Dwight Clark makes the NFL's most famous catch in a 1981 playoff game.

Francisco. The 49ers went on to win Super Bowl XVI that season and, eventually, five NFL titles in 14 years.

Center

The center is appropriately named because he's in the middle of the action on every play. He is the man who snaps, or hikes, the ball to the quarterback. Then he must be strong enough and quick enough to withstand the immediate crush of a defender who often is lined up directly across from him.

The center's responsibilities go even beyond snapping the ball and blocking. He is responsible for calling signals to the offensive line so they know what player to block on a given play.

Chain Gang

Formally called the "chain crew," these are the people on the sidelines who track the spot of the ball on the field and the distance needed for a first down.

One member of the chain gang holds a brightly colored pole that signals where a set of downs begins. That pole is connected to another pole by exactly 10 yards of chain. The second pole marks the spot a team needs to reach to gain a first down.

continued on page 48

Chicago Bears

As charter members of the NFL, the Bears have built a tradition of excellence and a loyal fan following rivaled only by that of another long-time franchise, the Green Bay Packers. In fact, Chicago's

■ Walter "Sweetness" Payton, superstar!

nine league championships (entering 2007) are second in NFL history only to the Packers' 12 titles.

The Bears' franchise actually began as the Decatur Staleys in the first season of the newly formed NFL (then called the American Professional Football Association) in 1920. The next year, the club moved to Chicago. After one season called the Staleys, the franchise became the Bears in 1921. It was common practice at the time to name a city's football team after its baseball team. But owner and founder George Halas reasoned that "Bears" were bigger and more ferocious than "Cubs."

Halas was one of the most influential figures in NFL history, and helped shape the nature of the league with many of his ideas. He also was an excellent player and an enormously successful head coach who spent four separate 10-year stints on Chicago's sidelines. By the time he retired in 1967, he had amassed 324 career coaching victories—a record that stood more than a quarter century before Don Shula broke it.

In their early existence, the Bears came to be known as the "Monsters of the Midway" after the city's famous Midway Park. The name has stuck over the years, and has come to represent the rugged defensive style of play that has become a club staple.

That is not to say that the franchise has

been lacking offensive stars. Its most famous players on that side of the ball have been quarterback Sid Luckman and running backs Gale Sayers and Walter Payton, all members of the Pro Football Hall of Fame.

Luckman quarterbacked the Bears more than half a century ago (1939–1950), but he remains the club's all-time leader in career passing yards (14,686) and touchdown passes (137).

Sayers was a dynamic halfback and kick returner who burst onto the scene by scoring 22 touchdowns as a rookie in 1965. Though injuries limited him to only seven seasons, he amassed 9,435 combined net yards in his short career, and at 34 years old in 1977 became the youngest player ever inducted into the Pro Football Hall of Fame.

Payton followed soon after Sayers, playing 13 seasons from 1975 to 1987. When he retired, he was the NFL's all-time leader with 16,726 career rushing yards (he remains second on that list).

Still, it is defense for which the Bears are known, and their history is dotted with fierce defensive stars such as Pro Football Hall of Famers Bronko Nagurski, Bill George, Dick Butkus, and Mike Singletary. From his middle linebacker position, Singletary anchored perhaps the most dominating defensive squad in recent NFL history, the famous "46 Defense" that carried Chicago to a league championship in the 1985 season.

The Bears' 46–10 rout of the New England Patriots in Super Bowl XX that year marked their ninth and, to date, final NFL title. But recent Bears' teams have brought back memories of that 1985 squad. Since Lovie Smith took over as head coach in 2004, the Bears have featured a ball-hawking, big-play defense worthy of the "Monsters of the Midway" moniker. In 2005, that unit allowed fewer points than any other team in the NFL (202). In 2006, Chicago kept rolling with 15 wins and a berth in Super Bowl XLI.

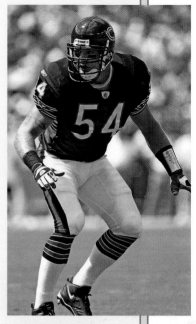

■ *Brian Urlacher leads a powerful Bears' defense.*

CHICAGO BEARS

CONFERENCE: NFC

DIVISION: NORTH

TEAM COLORS: NAVY BLUE, ORANGE, AND WHITE

STADIUM (CAPACITY): SOLDIER FIELD (61,500)

ALL-TIME RECORD: 686–499–42

NFL CHAMPIONSHIPS (MOST RECENT): 9 (1985)

Player-coach George Halas led the Bears in the 1933 title game.

A third member of the chain gang holds another pole that tracks where the ball is on every down—which not only is helpful to players, fans, and announcers, but also to the officials in case a penalty makes it necessary to mark off yards from the previous spot. The third pole also has a number at the top of it that the chain gang member changes after every play to signify the down.

Chicago Bears

Please see pages 46-47.

Chicago College All-Star Game

The Chicago College All-Star Game was an annual preseason exhibition game pitting the defending NFL champions against a team of all-stars from different colleges. It was held in Chicago each year from 1934 to 1976 (except in 1974).

In 42 games, the pro teams won 31, lost 9, and tied 2. The final game, played in July of 1976, was a 24–0 victory for the Super Bowl X-champion Pittsburgh Steelers.

Chicago Stadium

Chicago Stadium was the site of the first indoor NFL game: a preseason contest in 1930 between the Chicago Bears and the Chicago Cardinals. In 1932, the arena also hosted one of the most significant games in NFL history.

When a severe blizzard hit the city of Chicago that December, an important end-of-season game between the Bears and the Portsmouth Spartans—the winner of the game would be the league champion—was forced to the indoor arena. The field was not long enough (it was only 80 yards, so every time a team crossed midfield it was sent back 20 yards) or wide enough, but here are a few of the ways that the game impacted NFL history:

➤ Because the field was too narrow and surrounded by hockey boards, when a ball carrier was tackled too close to the outer boundaries, the ball was moved

10 yards closer to the middle of the field for the next snap. Thus, the first hash-marks—today, they are the small, white lines in one-yard increments between which each play begins—were created. The idea made so much sense that the league adopted the rule the next year.

➤ The game convinced NFL owners to split the league into divisions in 1933 and create the first, official NFL Championship Game.

➤ The Bears won 9–0 in large part because of a controversial touchdown pass. At the time, all passes had to be from at least five yards behind the line of scrimmage. Portsmouth argued that Chicago's touchdown pass was closer to the line than that. Two years later, the NFL legalized forward passing from anywhere behind the line of scrimmage.

The stadium was built on the site of the old Cleveland Stadium, which was the home of the original Browns for 50 seasons. Cleveland Browns Stadium has a natural grass field and seats 73,300.

Clipping

Clipping is an illegal block from behind and below the waist. It is a 15-yard penalty. Clipping most often is called on plays that involve changes of possession and thus features players blocking in the open field, like kickoff returns, punt returns, and interception and fumble returns.

Coffin Corner

This is a slang term for the corners created at each end of the field where the out of bounds line intersects the goal

continued on page 52

Cincinnati Bengals

Please see pages 50-51.

Cleveland Browns

Please see pages 54-55.

Cleveland Browns Stadium

Cleveland Browns Stadium has been the home of the Cleveland Browns since the franchise re-entered the NFL in 1999.

▮ *In this picture, the coffin corners are near the Broncos end zone.*

Cincinnati Bengals

After decades of little success, the Bengals have come to life in the 2000s, transforming themselves behind one of the NFL's most exciting offenses and big-play defenses. Cincinnati won its first division championship in 15 years in 2005.

■ *Anderson took the Bengals to a Super Bowl.*

The Bengals began as an expansion team in the American Football League (AFL) in 1968. Their first coach was the legendary Paul Brown, who already was a member of the Pro Football Hall of Fame after turning the Cleveland Browns into an NFL powerhouse the previous decade. The Bengals won the AFC Central Division with a modest 8–6 record in the first year of the "new" NFL in 1970, then making two more trips to the postseason in the 1970s.

A run of bad seasons ended in 1981, when the team won an AFC-best 12 games. With a coolly efficient quarterback in Ken Anderson, an all-star receiver in Cris Collinsworth, and one of the best offensive linemen of all time in tackle Anthony Muñoz, head coach Forrest Gregg's squad went on to win AFC title and reach the Super Bowl for the first time before falling to the San Francisco 49ers in game XVI.

Cincinnati didn't immediately build on that success, but later in the decade, Sam Wyche was the head coach when the Bengals played the 49ers again in Super Bowl XXIII in the 1988 season. Boomer Esiason was Cincinnati's quarterback. Rookie running back named Ickey Woods took the NFL by storm with his entertaining end-zone dance (the "Ickey Shuffle"). But San Francisco won again, scoring a touchdown in the final minute to come from behind.

■ *Carson Palmer leads today's Bengals.*

After nine wins in 1990 was enough to win the Central Division, the Bengals fell into a bad streak. They won fewer games in the decade than any other team in the NFL, and several seasons featured last-place finishes. Not even the high draft choices such poor records brought could help Cincinnati rise from its awful depths.

Finally, the Bengals roared to the AFC North title in 2005 behind a quick-strike offense that featured quarterback Carson Palmer, the top overall pick in the 2003 draft, passing to star wide receivers Chad Johnson and T.J. Houshmandzadeh.

Palmer passed for a club-record 32 touchdowns that year while Johnson set a club mark with 1,432 receiving yards. When the team wanted to keep the ball on the ground, though, it could do that with equal effectiveness as Rudi Johnson ran behind a cohesive and experienced offensive line. Rudi Johnson gained 1,458 yards, another club record. On defense, head coach Marvin Lewis built a ball-hawking unit that pressured the opposing quarterback and forced lots of turnovers.

That all added up to an 11–5 record during the regular season, earning Cincinnati its first division title since the 1990 squad. The Bengals' NFL title hopes were dashed by division-rival and eventual Super Bowl-champion Pittsburgh in the opening round of the playoffs. Palmer suffered a serious knee injury while completing a 66-yard pass to Chris Henry on the team's second offensive play of the game. Though backup Jon Kitna played admirably, he could not fend off a 31–17 defeat.

Palmer worked hard to rehabilitate from the injured ligaments he suffered that day and was back in the lineup in time for the 2006 season opener.

CINCINNATI BENGALS

CONFERENCE: AFC

DIVISION: NORTH

TEAM COLORS: BLACK, ORANGE, AND WHITE

STADIUM (CAPACITY): PAUL BROWN STADIUM (65,578)

ALL-TIME RECORD: 266–342–1

NFL CHAMPIONSHIPS (MOST RECENT): NONE

line. Punters often try to kick near the coffin corner (inside the 20-yard line).

Coin Toss

Before every game, the coin toss is held at midfield by the referee with the team captains. The winner of the coin toss (heads or tails, visitor calls which) gets to choose whether his team will receive the ball first or defend a particular end of the field. In the NFL, the decision almost always is to take the ball, since the choice switches to the other team for the second half. (The teams switch ends each quarter.)

Coldest Games

Bart Starr's 1-yard quarterback sneak with 13 seconds remaining gave the Green Bay Packers a 21–17 victory over the visiting Dallas Cowboys in frigid conditions in the 1967 NFL Championship Game. The temperature at kickoff for the game, which has come to be known as the "Ice Bowl," was 13 degrees below zero. It is officially the coldest game on record on league his-

tory. See the box below for more.

Comebacks, Greatest

Playing at home in the opening round of the 1992 playoffs, the Buffalo Bills fell behind the Houston Oilers 35–3 in the third quarter, sending many of their fans to the exits. Remarkably, Buffalo rallied to tie the game at 38–38, then won in overtime, 41–38. It is most points any NFL team ever has come back from to win a game. The box on page 53 shows the greatest regular-season comebacks ever.

Completion

A pass attempt by an offensive player that is caught by another offensive player. Almost always, it's by the quarterback to a wide receiver, running back, or tight end, but it can be among any two eligible players. (Or, in extremely rare cases, a quarterback completes a pass that is tipped at the line of scrimmage to himself!) An "incompletion" or "incomplete pass" is a pass attempt that is not caught.

COLDEST GAMES

TEMP (F)	WIND-CHILL	DATE	SITE
–13 degrees	–48 degrees	Dec. 31, 1967	Green Bay, Wisconsin
NFL Championship Game: Green Bay 21, Dallas 17			
–9 degrees	–59 degrees	January 10, 1982	Cincinnati, Ohio
AFC Championship Game: Cincinnati 27, San Diego 7			
0 degrees	–32 degrees	January 15, 1994	Orchard Park, New York
AFC Divisional Playoff Game: Buffalo 29, L.A. Raiders 23			

Clark, Earl "Dutch"

Dutch Clark was not reportedly had very poor eyesight. And he apparently didn't have a strong throwing arm. But Clark was a first-team all-league choice six times and was among the initial inductees to the Pro Football Hall of Fame when the shrine opened in 1963.

What Clark did possess was remarkable intelligence and football savvy. As a Single-Wing tailback for the Portsmouth Spartans (1931–32) and Detroit Lions (1934–38)—the club moved after the 1933 season—he was the franchise's top field general. He led the team in rushing, passing, and scoring in 1934, then guided the franchise to its first NFL championship in 1935. His first-quarter touchdown run was the key play of the Lions' 26–7 victory over the Giants.

The last of the NFL's dropkick specialists (a drop kick is a ball that hits the ground before it is booted), Clark led the league in scoring three times.

■ *Dutch Clark was an all-around star.*

Cornerback

A cornerback's main job is to cover opposing pass catchers. He generally lines up directly in front of the opposing team's wide receiver on one side of the field or the other (one cornerback on each side).

A cornerback must be fast enough to guard a wide receiver, who often is among the fastest players on the field. Cornerbacks have to be fast while running backward, so they can watch the quarterback, too. A good cornerback also has to be strong enough to help out with stopping the run. That might mean abandoning coverage of the wide receiver when he sees that it is a running play, or it might mean lining up closer to the line of scrimmage in run support.

Along with safeties, cornerbacks are considered part of the secondary, or the "defensive backfield."

continued on page 56

GREATEST COMEBACKS

DEFICIT	DATE	TEAMS
28	Dec. 7, 1980	San Francisco 38, New Orleans 35
The 49ers trailed 35–7 in the third quarter.		
26	Sept. 21, 1997	Buffalo 37, Indianapolis 35
The Bills trailed 26–0 in the second quarter.		
25	Nov. 8, 1987	St. Louis 31, Tampa Bay 28

■ *QB Otto Graham and Paul Brown*

Cleveland Browns

The Cleveland Browns really are a tale of two franchises: The first began in the All-America Football Conference in 1946, then joined the NFL in 1950; the second started as an expansion franchise in 1999 after the original Browns moved to Baltimore following the 1995 season. The first version of the Browns had considerable success. The second? Not so much.

The disjointed history of the Browns is the result of an unusual sequence of events in the 1990s. Though the club enjoyed a large and vocal following in Cleveland, team owner Art Modell announced midway through the 1995 season that he would be moving the club to Baltimore in time for the 1996 season. The Browns' loyalists were stunned. And because the team had such a loyal fan base, the NFL took the unique step of keeping the team's history and records in Cleveland. The franchise in Baltimore, though featuring many of the same players and front office personnel who were with the Browns in 1995, would start from scratch in 1996. And when the league awarded an expansion franchise for Cleveland in 1999, that first-year club already would come with an extensive history!

The original Browns won the AAFC championship all four seasons of that league's existence. In fact, they may have hastened the demise of the AAFC because there was little suspense among the paying fans as to who would win the title each year. Paul Brown, the club's original head coach and the man for whom the franchise was named, was responsible for many innovations in pro football, such as calling plays from the sidelines and grading players based on film study.

Brown's methods were an unqualified success in the AAFC, but when the club (along with the defunct league's San Francisco 49ers and Baltimore Colts) joined the NFL in 1950, most pro football experts figured Cleveland would meet its match, starting with its opening game against defending-champion Philadelphia. Instead, in what was then considered a stunning upset, the Browns routed the Eagles 35–10. Cleveland had announced its arrival in the new league.

The Browns, featuring future Pro Football Hall of Fame members such as quarterback Otto Graham, running back Marion Motley, wide receiver Dante Lavelli, and end Len Ford, never let up, rolling to the NFL championship. In a bit of irony, they defeated the Los Angeles Rams, the team that had left Cleveland in 1945 and paved the way for the Browns' arrival the following year, in the 1950 title game.

Cleveland went on to play in the next five NFL Championship Games, too, winning twice. By the time Graham retired following a 38–14 rout of the Rams in the 1955 game, he had played in 10 consecutive league championship games (AAFC and NFL)—a standard of excellence for a quarterback that may never be matched.

Then in the late 1950s and early 1960s, Jim Brown set the standard for NFL running backs. He led the league in rushing eight times in nine seasons before retiring at the top of his game following the 1965 season.

In 1970, as part of the merger agreement between the AFL and the NFL, the Browns joined the Pittsburgh Steelers, the Baltimore Colts, and the 10 existing AFL franchises to form the 13-team American Football Conference (AFC). Though Cleveland has featured some outstanding players such as quarterbacks Brian Sipe and Bernie Kosar, the Browns have not won a conference title.

And since re-joining the league in 1999, the Browns have posted just one winning season. That came in 2002, when head coach Butch Davis led Cleveland to a 9–7 record and a wild-card playoff berth. The team has not returned to the postseason since. In 2005, former Patriots assistant Romeo Crennel was hired to take over the club.

■ *Charlie Frye now leads the Browns' offense.*

CLEVELAND BROWNS

CONFERENCE: AFC

DIVISION: NORTH

**TEAM COLORS:
BROWN, ORANGE, AND WHITE**

**STADIUM (CAPACITY):
CLEVELAND BROWNS STADIUM (73,300)**

**ALL-TIME RECORD:
425–374–10**

**NFL CHAMPIONSHIPS
(MOST RECENT):
4 (1964)**

Cover 2

"Cover 2" is a standard pass defense in the NFL. Every NFL team uses some version of this formation, and you'll often hear announcers talk about it. Basically, it means that there are two safeties in the defensive backfield, each of whom is responsible for covering one side of the field.

The Cover 2 is used with either a 4-3 (four down linemen and three linebackers) or a 3-4 (three down linemen and four linebackers) defense. Two cornerbacks then cover the outside wide receivers with help from the two safeties deep.

■ *Bill Cowher: Intense player, intense coach.*

Cowher, Bill

With his steely glare and set jaw, Bill Cowher patrolled the sideline as the Steelers' head coach from 1992 through 2006. Along with Pro Football Hall of Fame coach Chuck Noll, he was one of only two Pittsburgh head coaches from 1969 through 2006.

Cowher developed his trademark intensity as an NFL linebacker for six seasons (1979–1984) for the Philadelphia Eagles and Cleveland Browns. He began his coaching career as an assistant with the Browns in 1985 and was just 34 years old when he was named to succeed Noll as the Steelers' head coach in January of 1992.

In only his fourth season at the helm in 1995, the 38-year-old Cowher became the youngest coach ever to lead his team to the Super Bowl, though Pittsburgh lost game XXX to Dallas. Still, the Steelers reached the postseason six more times in the next 10 years, capped with an appearance in Super Bowl XL in the 2005 season. That time, Cowher's club downed Seattle 21–10 to win Pittsburgh's record-tying fifth Super Bowl, but its first since 1979. He retired following the 2006 season to spend more time with his family.

Creekmur, Lou

Lou Creekmur was a fixture on the offensive lines of the great Detroit Lions' teams that won three NFL championships during the 1950s. Creekmur began his career as a guard in 1950 and later was all-league at tackle and middle (later called nose) guard as well. He was inducted into the Pro Football Hall of Fame in 1996.

Crossbar

The horizontal bar of the bright gold goal posts, the crossbar is positioned 10 feet above the ground. The vertical posts, which are 18 feet, 6 inches apart and are connected to the crossbar, are called "uprights."

A successful field goal or extra point attempt goes over the crossbar and between the uprights.

Csonka, Larry

Larry Csonka was a bruising fullback who was a key part of the Dolphins' championship teams of the early 1970s. In 1972, he helped Miami have the only unbeaten, untied season in NFL history. The next year, he was named the most valuable player of the Dolphins' 24–7 victory over Minnesota in Super Bowl VIII when he rushed for a then-record 145 yards.

Csonka packed 237 pounds on his 6-3 frame. His brute strength and sure hands, combined with the efforts of fellow running backs Jim Kiick and Mercury Morris, helped Miami rely on a ball-control offense. In 1971, Csonka became the first player in club history to run for more than

◼ *Csonka used brute strength to succeed.*

1,000 yards in a season (1,051). He topped 1,000 yards in each of the next two seasons, and Miami reached the Super Bowl all three years.

Csonka, who later played in the World Football League and for the NFL's New York Giants, was inducted into the Pro Football Hall of Fame in 1987.

Dallas Cowboys

Though the Dallas Cowboys have been a part of the NFL for just more than half of the league's history, they are one of the most successful teams all-time. Sometimes known as "America's Team" for their nationwide popularity, the Cowboys are one of only three teams to have won five Super Bowls. They had an un-

■ *Roger Staubach led Dallas to two titles.*

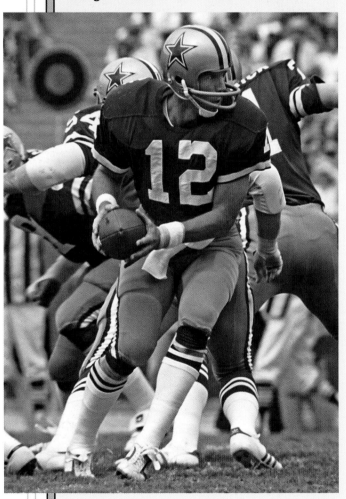

matched streak of winning records every year from 1966 through 1985. And though they struggled for their first decade of existence, they have since boasted an array of some of the finest players of all time.

In January, 1960, the NFL granted an expansion franchise to a pair of Dallas businessmen, Clint Murchison and Bedford Wynne. They quickly made their most impor- tant (and successful) business decision: They made Tom Landry the head coach. Landry was a former player and an assistant coach. He would become the face of the club for nearly 30 years.

The Cowboys were not very good in their early years. In fact, they didn't even win a game in their first season, 1960, going 0-11-1. By the 1970 season, they had im- proved enough to win they their first NFC championship. However, they lost Super Bowl V to the Baltimore Colts on a last-minute field goal. The rest of the 1970s would see them solidly among the league's top teams. Led by future Hall of Fame quarterback Roger Staubach, the Cowboys won Super Bowl VI to capture their first NFL title. Four years later, the team again made it to Super Bowl X, only to fall to Pittsburgh amid that team's own dynasty of titles. Dallas bounced back to win Super Bowl XII, led by a power- ful defense. However, in Super Bowl XIII, the Steelers once again had the Cowboys' number. Still, the Cowboys had played in five Super Bowls in eight years, an unmatched run of excellence.

However, the 1980s were just about the opposite for Dallas. Staubach retired and the team did not excel. A major change occurred in 1989 when oilman (and former college football player) Jerry Jones bought the team. Jones made a huge move by letting Landry go; many fans were shocked that the new owner would remove such a legend, but they soon changed their tune. Like Landry, new coach Jimmy Johnson had a rough start (1-15 in 1989), but by 1992 had built his team around quarterback Troy Aikman and led the Cowboys to a dominating 52-17 victory over Buffalo in Super Bowl XXVII. They repeated as champs the following year and made it three titles in four years by winning Super Bowl XXX. That last title came under the direction of former University of Oklahoma coach Barry Switzer, who had taken over from Johnson in 1994.

The Cowboys of the 1990s were one of the NFL's greatest dynasties. Along with Aikman, they boasted record-setting running back Emmitt Smith and high-flying receiver Michael Irvin. As the team kept winning, it attracted fans from around the country. The nickname "America's Team," which came into use in the 1970s, means fans everywhere looked to the big white Cowboys' star in their search for football excellence. The Dallas Cowboys cheerleaders also became nationally famous, appearing in movies and on TV shows. (Here's a fun bit of trivia: When the team was founded in 1960, it was almost named the Rangers instead of the Cowboys.)

Three-time Super Bowl champion Bill Parcells took over as head coach in 2003 and brought lots of headlines but no championships to Dallas. He made Tony Romo the starter in 2006 and Dallas made the playoffs. Though "America's Team" is no longer the powerhouse it once was, its long-time fans always hope. As they love to say in Big D, "How 'bout them Cowboys!"

DALLAS COWBOYS

CONFERENCE: NFC

DIVISION: EAST

TEAM COLORS: SILVER AND BLUE

STADIUM (CAPACITY): TEXAS STADIUM (65,529)

ALL-TIME RECORD (THROUGH 2006): 433–322–6

NFL CHAMPIONSHIPS (MOST RECENT): 5 (1995)

■ *Running back Julius Jones.*

Davis, Al

No team in any sport reflects the image of its owner more than the Raiders. From the 1960s through the 2000s, the Raiders have risen and fallen under the leadership of Al Davis, who carries the title of Managing General Partner.

The Raiders always have oozed an "outlaw" attitude just like their famous owner. But behind the attitude and on the other side of the team's Silver and Black "pirate" colors are a lot of great football men. For example, John Madden was the Raiders' coach from 1969–1978. Team executive Al LoCasale was Davis' right-hand man for three decades. On the field, the left side of the Raiders' line in the 1970s, guard Gene Upshaw and tackle Art Shell, both went on to the Hall of Fame and then to other high achievements in the game. The team's—and Davis'—motto is "Commitment to Excellence."

Davis and the Raiders had their greatest success in the 1970s. Oakland won 112 games from 1970–980. Only Dallas (117) won more games in that period; the Raiders and the Cowboys were the only teams not to have a losing year. Pittsburgh won four Super Bowls (IX, X, XIII, XIV) while Oakland (XI, XV), Dallas (VI, XII), and Miami (VII, VIII) won two each. Oakland also lost three other AFC Championship Games in the decade.

Davis' eye for talent was legend. He cared about a player's potential not about where he came from, and about how a player played on the field, not how he looked off of it. Davis' Raiders have often been among football's most colorful characters. The team's fans—the team played in Oakland from 1960–1981 and since 1995, and in Los Angeles from 1982–1994—often had the same crazy look.

■ *Davis has been the heart and soul of the Raiders since 1963.*

The magic of Silver and Black has been largely missing in the last two decades. In their last 11 seasons in Los Angeles the Raiders made it to only one AFC Championship Game. In 12 seasons in Oakland since 1995, the Raiders lost the 2000 Championship Game and were thrashed by Tampa Bay in Super Bowl XXXVII.

LoCasale thinks the Silver and Black uniform—a Davis design when he arrived in Oakland to coach the Raiders at age 33 in 1963—is crucial to the team's bad guy reputation.

"Good guys wear white hats," LoCasale says. "We didn't want to be good guys. We wanted to scare people. This is football, after all."

Dead ball

When a play is whistled over—that is, the officials stop the play—the ball is dead. That means it can't be advanced by either team or put in play until the start of the next play. The term "dead ball penalty" means a foul committed while the ball is not in play, usually unsportsmanlike conduct.

Defense

The team on the field that is trying to stop the team with the ball. The defensive team is usually broken down into three sections: defensive line, linebackers, and defensive secondary. Players on defense are good tacklers and are often very fast and aggressive.

Defensive back

One of the players on defense who is part of the defensive secondary. Safeties and cornerbacks are the two types of defensive backs. The main job of defensive backs is to cover opposing pass receivers. Defensive backs also try to tackle any player running with the ball. Defensive backs are usually very fast and quick; they can often run as fast backward as many people can run forward.

Defensive coordinator

The assistant coach charged with organizing his team's defense. The

Davis, Willie

A five-time Pro Bowl player and two-time Super Bowl champion, Willie Davis was one of the dominating defensive players of the 1960s. After playing college football at Grambling State and two seasons with the Cleveland Browns, Davis joined the Green Bay Packers in 1960. He helped turn the Packers into one of the NFL's greatest dynasties. They won five NFL titles while Davis was with the team, including the first two Super Bowls. Davis was big (6-3 and 245 pounds), fast, and smart. He was as much of a leader on the field as he was a fierce tackler. Playing most often as a defensive end on the left side, he was also durable. In his 12 seasons in the NFL, he didn't miss one game due to injury.

Following his NFL career, Davis became a successful radio station owner and businessman. He was named to the Pro Football Hall of Fame in 1981.

■ *Willie Davis in a posed action photo; yes, he wore a helmet in games.*

Dawson, Len

Len Dawson had a slow beginning to his Hall of Fame career, but he made up for it by becoming one of the best passers of the 1960s. Drafted by Pittsburgh in 1957, he became a starter later in the AFL and led the Dallas Texans to the title in 1962. In 1966, Kansas City (the team had moved from Dallas and become the Chiefs) and Dawson won the AFL crown again and with it a berth in the new Super Bowl against the NFL champion Green Bay Packers. The Packers showed them who was boss, however, winning 35-10. Dawson kept going, however, continuing as one of the game's most accurate passers (he would lead the league in completion percentage nine times in his career).

By the time of Super Bowl IV, he and the Chiefs were ready to win it all. They defeated Minnesota 23-7 and Dawson was named the MVP of the game.

Dawson retired after the 1975 season and became a longtime football broadcaster. He was named to the Hall of Fame in 1987.

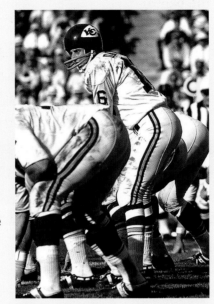
■ *Dawson in Super Bowl IV.*

coordinator, working with the head coach, chooses which players will play in which formations. He makes up a game plan to attack the opposing team's weaknesses and protect against its strengths.

Defensive end

Two defensive ends line up on each play, one on each side of the defensive line opposite the offense. The ends start with one hand down and charge forward at the snap of the ball. Most defensive ends are very quick, but also very big. This combination can make them hard to stop. Their main goal is to sack the quarterback or at least make him hurry his throw. On running plays, defensive ends try to tackle the runner or at least occupy a blocker so that a teammate can come up and make the tackle.

Defensive line

The defensive players directly opposite the ball on the line of scrimmage. Most defensive lines have three or four players on them. In a three-man line, there is a nose tackle in the middle and two defensive ends. In a four-man line, there are two tackles in the middle, with an end on either side of them. The defensive line's main job is to attack the quarterback if he goes back to pass. The defensive line players use a variety of techniques to try to get past the blockers on the offensive line. On running plays, they try to stop the ballcarrier soon after he gets the ball to keep him from "breaking through the line" and gaining additional yards.

Defensive tackle

The central players on the defensive line are the defensive tackles. In a three-man line, they are called "nose tackles."

Delay of game

A five-yard penalty on the offense caused by taking too much time between plays. In the NFL, the offense must start a new play within 40 seconds. A team gets a fresh 40 seconds after the previous play ends. In some cases, this "play clock" won't start right away after that play. In those cases, teams have 25 seconds to start a new play. A large digital clock in each stadium helps players—most importantly the quarterback who must call for the snap— and officials keep track of the time.

Denver Broncos

Please see pages 64-65.

Detroit Lions

Please see pages 66-67.

Denver Mile High Stadium

The original home of the Denver Broncos seats 76,082 orange-wearing football fans. The stadium got its famous nickname from, just as the city does, its elevation above sea level. The city of Denver is more than 5,000 feet up in the Rocky Mountains, about a mile above sea level. Visiting teams were sometimes at a disadvantage as they are not used to the thinner air. The Broncos played in the stadium from 1960 through 2000.

■ *Denver's new stadium, Invesco Field, still featured a rearing stallion.*

Denver Broncos

One of the AFL's original teams, the Broncos came close to success several times in their first three decades, but never grabbed the brass ring. A victory in Super Bowl XXXII, however, finally moved them from the ranks of "almost" to "champion."

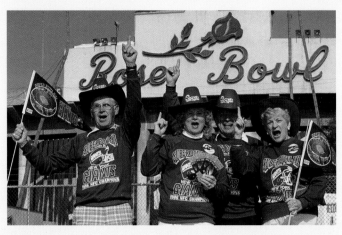

■ *Young or old, Denver's fans love their team!*

The Broncos were one of the original teams in the American Football League, beginning play in 1960. Though they won their first game, that was a rare highlight. The team went 14 years before they put together a winning season. Among the few memories of the Broncos' early seasons worth mentioning are the ugliest socks in NFL history, with vertical brown stripes; a 1967 preseason victory over Detroit, the first by an AFL team over an NFL team (though, of course, it didn't really count!); and the play of Marlin Briscoe in 1968, the first African-American to see more than spot action at quarterback.

In the mid-1970s, coach Red Miller led the team to its first success. The key was its "Orange Crush" defense that stifled opponents. On offense, former Cowboys quarterback Craig Morton provided veteran leadership. In 1977, the Broncos won their first AFC title and earned a spot in Super Bowl XII. However, they were steamrolled by Dallas, Morton's old team.

In 1983, the Broncos' sagging fortunes took a sharp upward turn with the trade for superstar college quarterback John Elway. An athletic, strong-armed leader, Elway made the Broncos his own, leading them to six seasons with 10 or more victories in his first 10 years with the team. They won AFC titles in 1986 (see "The Drive"), 1987, and 1989, though they lost all three

DENVER BRONCOS

CONFERENCE: **AFC**

DIVISION: **WEST**

TEAM COLORS:
ORANGE AND BLUE

STADIUM (CAPACITY):
**INVESCO FIELD
AT MILE HIGH (76,125)**

ALL-TIME RECORD:
(THROUGH 2006):
388–342–10

NFL CHAMPIONSHIPS
(MOST RECENT):
2 (1998)

ensuing Super Bowls. Fans worried that, although Elway was among the best players in the league, he couldn't "win the big one."

Through the 1990s, Denver improved steadily. First, Mike Shanahan, one of the game's brightest young offensive minds, took over as head coach. Then, with the addition of running back Terrell Davis in 1995, Elway had a powerful weapon to balance his passing game. Two years later, the Broncos headed back to the Super Bowl, hoping to end a four-game losing streak in the big game. Thanks to Davis' 157-yard MVP performance, Elway and the Broncos could finally hold up the Lombardi Trophy as NFL champs.

They made it two in a row in 1998, as Elway moved farther up the all-time passing charts and led the team to a 14-2 record, its best ever. With 2,008 yards, Davis became the fourth player ever to top the 2,000-yard barrier. Denver romped through the playoffs and then Elway capped off his amazing career by winning

the MVP of Super Bowl XXXIII, which Denver won easily over Atlanta.

Elway retired after that game, with his next stop Canton, Ohio, and the Pro Football Hall of Fame in 2004. The Broncos have made the playoffs several times since 1998, but have not reached the Super Bowl again.

■ *Strong-armed John Elway led Denver to two Super Bowl titles.*

■ *Barry Sanders was a dazzling runner.*

Detroit Lions

Though they have been around for nearly all of the NFL's more than 80 years, the Detroit Lions have not been on top of the league for nearly half a century. They had some success in their distant past, but recent seasons have not seen much winning in the Motor City.

The team began in 1930 as the Portsmouth Spartans, based in the Ohio city of that name. The big name for the team in those days was quarterback Dutch Clark. In 1932, Clark and the Spartans tied for first place with the Chicago Bears. The teams scheduled a playoff, but a bad snowstorm forced the game to be played indoors. It was the first regular-season indoor game in NFL history. The field in the Chicago Stadium was shorter and narrower. To keep the players from running into the hockey boards, the ball was placed near the middle of the field after each play. The idea of the "hashmarks" where the ball was replaced caught on and became a regular part of NFL fields.

The team moved to Detroit for the 1934 season and became the Lions. They won their first NFL title in 1935 as Clark continued to be one of the league's best all-around players. The 1940s featured several top players, including 1944 league MVP Frank Sinkwich, but not much in the way of team success.

The addition of two players in 1950 changed the team's fortunes and led to Detroit's greatest run of success. Quarterback Bobby Layne and running back Doak Walker would help the Lions reach the NFL title game five times, winning three. The first in this run came in 1952 over the mighty Cleveland Browns. The Lions made it two straight in 1953, scoring a late touchdown to beat the Browns 17-16. Cleveland got its revenge in 1954, however, smashing Detroit 56-10. In 1957, backup QB Tobin Rote took over for an injured Layne, while the massive and fierce linebacker Joe Schimidt anchored the defense on the Lions' way to another NFL title. However, that was the last gasp for the Lions in the 1900s. Though they made the playoffs occasionally, they never reached the Super Bowl and have only won one playoff game since (in 1991).

The team was bought by Henry Clay Ford in 1964 and the famous automotive family still owns the team.

Perhaps the greatest player in Lions history joined the team in 1988. Heisman Trophy-winning running back Barry Sanders led the NFC in rushing in his first season. It was the start of one of the league's greatest careers.

■ *Receiver Roy Williams is a current Lions' star.*

Sanders played 10 years and topped 1,000 yards in each of them. He won five NFL rushing titles. In 1997, he became the third player in NFL history (after O.J. Simpson and Eric Dickerson) to reach 2,000 yards; Sanders's total was 2,053 yards. The Lions could never match the great back's success, however, and only rarely reached playoff status until Sanders retired suddenly in 1998.

In recent years, the Lions have struggled to find an identity, changing coaches several times and not posting a winning record since the 2000 season.

DETROIT LIONS

CONFERENCE: **NFC**

DIVISION: **NORTH**

TEAM COLORS: **BLUE AND SILVER**

STADIUM (CAPACITY): **FORD FIELD (64,50))**

ALL-TIME RECORD: (THROUGH 2006): **488–554–32**

NFL CHAMPIONSHIPS (MOST RECENT): **4 (1957)**

Dickerson, Eric

For most of the 1980s, there were few more exciting moments in football than when Eric Dickerson got the ball behind the line of scrimmage and got up a head of steam heading downfield. A big man , blessed with great speed and vision, Dickerson set a single-season record of 2,105 yards in 1984 that stood through 2006.

After an All-America career at Southern Methodist University, Dickerson set a rookie record in his first season with the then-Los Angeles Rams, rushing for 1,804 yards. He set the all-time mark the next year and would gain at least 1,000 yards for a total of seven consecutive seasons. Dickerson was well-known for his high-stepping running style, his ability to see holes where it seemed none existed, and for the distinctive plastic goggles he wore while playing. He was traded to the Indianapolis Colts in 1987 and also saw time with the Raiders and Falcons.

When he retired in 1993, Dickerson

Ditka, Mike

Few men in NFL history were as tough as Mike Ditka and few had as much impact on their position. Before Ditka came along for the Chicago Bears in 1961, tight ends were almost exclusively blockers. While still blocking on many plays, Ditka turned the position into an offensive force. He had 12 touchdown catches as a rookie in 1961 and set a long-standing record for catches by a tight end with 75 in 1964. From then on, most teams boasted at least one big, strong player who could catch as well as he could block. Ditka helped the Bears win the 1963 NFL championship and was a five-time Pro Bowl selection. He later played for Dallas and helped the Cowboys win Super Bowl VI.

Most fans today, however, know Ditka as a coach. The fiery leader drove the Bears to a 15-1 record in 1985 followed by a resounding win in Super Bowl XX. He also gained fame in many advertisements and as a very opinionated TV commentator. Ditka briefly coached the New Orleans Saints in the late 1990s. He was named to the Hall of Fame in 1988.

■ *Ditka was the leader of "Da Bears."*

trailed only the great Walter Payton on the NFL's all-time rushing yardage list with a career total of 13,259 yards (both men's totals have since been surpassed). Dickerson was inducted into the Pro Football Hall of Fame in 1999.

Dillon, Corey

A standout running back for two teams in the early 2000s, Corey Dillon had seven 1,000 yard seasons through 2006. Dillon's best seasons were in 2000 for the Cincinnati Bengals, when he gained 1,435 yards, and 2004 with New England, when he set a career high with 1,635 yards. Dillon helped the Patriots make it to Super Bowl XXXIX after that season and scored a touchdown in New England's win over Philadelphia.

Dime

A term for a defensive formation that has six defensive backs on the field. The dime package is often used when the offense has to gain a large chunk of yardage on one play, which means they will most likely be attempting a long pass. The extra defensive backs (two more than usual) try to prevent this.

Dolphin Stadium

Home of the Miami Dolphins since 1987, the stadium has had many names. It was originally called Joe Robbie

■ *Corey Dillon rumbles for New England.*

Stadium after the team's longtime owner. The Pro Player company paid millions of dollars to name the stadium for itself from 1996 to 2004. It was renamed Dolphin Stadium for the 2005 season. Located in Miami, the orange-and-teal seats can hold 75,192 people. It was the site of Super Bowls XXIII, XXIX, XXXIV, and XLI.

Donovan, Art

 Though Art Donovan earned his place in the Pro Football Hall of Fame with

great play as a defensive tackle with the Baltimore Colts of the 1950s, he is more famous for his fun-loving personality. Donovan played in five straight Pro Bowls (1954-1958) and helped the Colts win the 1958 NFL championship. A smart and powerful player, he was equally talented at stopping the run as rushing the passer. After his playing career, the big, lovable Donovan was a regular on TV talk shows, telling humorous, goofy stories of his life on and off the field.

Doomsday Defense

During the Dallas Cowboys' great 1970s run (they played in five Super Bowls in eight years), the team's great strength was its defense. For their ability to shut down opposing teams, they earned this famous nickname.

Double coverage

When two defensive players cover one offensive receiver. This is usually done against the offense's top receiver.

Down

A single play from scrimmage in a football game. The offensive team gets four "downs" to gain at least 10 yards. If it fails, it loses the ball to the other team. If it gains 10 or more yards, it gets four more downs. Each time the offense snaps the ball and runs a play it uses up one down.

Draft

Each spring, the NFL holds a meeting at which NFL teams can choose college players to add to their roster. The order of the selections is determined by how the NFL teams finished the previous season. (The team with the poorest record chooses first.) However, draft picks can be traded, letting a higher-rated team pick near the top of the draft. A player chosen as the number-one overall draft pick is rewarded with a huge contract. The first draft was held in 1936.

Draw

A running play in which the quarterback pretends to drop back to pass, but then stops and hands off to a running back. The key to the play is the behavior of the offensive line. Those players have to act like they are pass-blocking and then shift suddenly to run blocking to help the running back find a hole in the line.

"The Drive"

In the 1986 AFC Championship Game in Cleveland, Denver quarterback John Elway led his team 98 yards in the final five minutes to score a dramatic tying touchdown. The Broncos went on to win the game in overtime and earn a place in Super Bowl XXI, where they lost to the New York Giants. Elway's march to the tie, however, became legendary, earning its simple nickname.

Dorsett, Tony

After winning the 1976 Heisman Trophy at the University of Pittsburgh, running back Tony Dorsett (pronounced "door-SETT") kept it going in the NFL. Drafted by the Cowboys, he began a streak of eight 1,000-yard totals in nine seasons. He won the 1982 NFL rushing title, earned four Pro Bowl selections, and helped the Cowboys win two NFC titles. Dorsett's most famous record can never be broken, only tied. He ripped off a 99-yard touchdown run during a Monday Night Football game in 1982. He was named to the Hall of Fame in 1994.

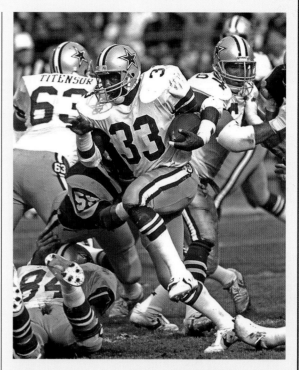

■ *Dorsett rushed for more than 10,000 yards.*

Drop back

The action of the quarterback after taking the snap from center and backing up to prepare to throw a pass.

Drop kick

Before placekicks, the method for attempting field goals and extra points was the drop kick. Taking the ball directly from the snap, the kicker dropped the ball straight down and kicked it at the instant it bounced back up from the ground. This was easier in the old days with the rounder ball then in use. The drop kick is still legal. Doug Flutie made a drop-kick extra point late in a 2005 game.

Duluth Eskimos

The Eskimos were an NFL team from 1923 through 1927. Their only real claim to fame, other than one of the coolest (pardon the pun) nicknames in league history, was their star running back Ernie Nevers, a Hall of Famer who spent the 1926 and 1927 seasons with them.

Dungy, Tony

An NFL coach for 11 years (through 2006) and former player, Dungy led the Indianapolis Colts to victory in Super Bowl XLI. He became, along with Chicago's Lovie Smith, the first African-American head coaches in a Super Bowl.

Jason Elam is one of the league's most dependable kickers.

from 2001 through 2005. He led them to an AFC East title in 2002, but struggled in the following years. Beginning in 2006, he took over as head coach of the Kansas City Chiefs. As a player, however, Edwards made a mark for his fine play as a defensive back for the Eagles. His most famous moment came in 1978 when he returned a botched handoff in the waning seconds of a game to win a game against the Giants. The play is known as the Miracle of the Meadowlands, after the location of Giants Stadium where it took place.

Edward Jones Dome

The home of the St. Louis Rams is located in downtown St. Louis, in the shadow of the famous Gateway Arch. Opened in 1995, it was first known as the Trans World Dome after the airline TWA. It was renamed the Edward Jones Dome in 2003 after a financial services company. The dome seats 66,000 people.

Edwards, Herm

Herm Edwards is familiar to today's fans for his work as a head coach. Edwards was the New York Jets' head coach

Elam, Jason

The longtime kicker for the Denver Broncos, Elam has been kicking field goals in the thin air in Denver since 1993. (At more than a mile above sea level, Denver's air is less dense and thus the ball moves through the air a bit more easily.) A steady performer, he had 10 seasons with at least 25 field goals through 2006. His greatest kick, however, came in 1998. On the final play of the first half in a game against Jacksonville, he kicked a 63-yard field goal, tying an all-time NFL record set in 1970.

Elway, John

Strong-armed, pigeon-toed, and as determined as any other quarterback in history, John Elway certainly deserves mention among the greatest players in football history. Elway was a star at Stanford and joined the Denver Broncos in 1983. He and the team struggled for a few years, but by 1986, they were in the Super Bowl. They would go on to play in—and lose—two more Super Bowls in the next four years.

Elway was often among the league leaders in passing and touchdown passes, He excelled in leading his team to come-from-behind victories. In 21 games, he engineered winning comebacks after Denver trailed with less than two minutes to play. His most famous comeback came in the 1986 AFC Championship Game. He led the Broncos 98 yards in less than five minutes, capping it off with a game-winning touchdown pass. They lost the ensuing Super Bowl to the Giants. Without a championship, Elway's career was still not complete.

Then, in the mid-1990s, Elway was joined by running back Terrell Davis and head coach Mike Shanahan. The trio led the Broncos to two straight Super Bowl victories, in XXXII and XXXIII. Elway was the MVP of the latter Super Bowl and retired in triumph, his legacy as a champion assured. He is in the top five all-time in attempts, completions, passing yards, and touchdown passes. He will be eligible for induction into the Hall of Fame in 2008.

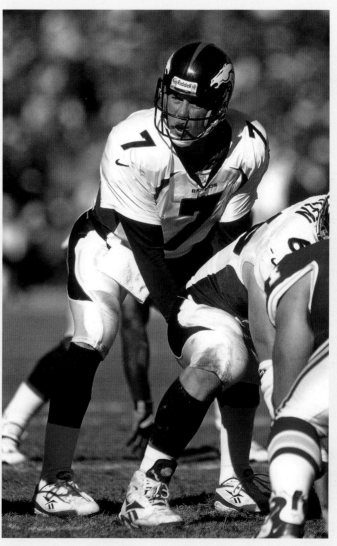

■ *John Elway is one of the best QBs of all time.*

Elephant Backfield

In general, a nickname for a formation that places extra-large players as running backs. When 300-pound defensive tackle William "The Refrigerator" Perry played running back, it was as an elephant. The most well-known Elephant Backfield played for the Los Angeles Rams in the early 1950s, when big men Dan Towler and Tank Younger often bulled over opposing defenses.

Encroachment

A defensive penalty that occurs when a defender crosses the line of scrimmage before the ball is snapped and makes contact with any offensive player. If he does not make contact, the penalty is called offside. In either case, the penalty is five yards.

End lines

The lines at the back of the end zone. They show the limit of the end zone. A player coming down with a pass and landing on the line is out of bounds, not in the end zone.

End zone

The 10-yard deep area at each end of the football field. The end zone is as wide as the field, and is the ultimate goal

■*In this photo of the field at Dolphin Stadium, the area with the three logos is the end zone.*

Ewbank, Weeb

A generally quiet and kind man, Ewbank was nonetheless tough enough to lead teams to two of the most dramatic victories in NFL history. With the help of star quarterback Johnny Unitas, Ewbank led the Baltimore Colts to the NFL title in 1958. They defeated the New York Giants in overtime in what has since been called "The Greatest Game Ever Played."

Ten years later, Ewbank had taken over the New York Jets of the AFL. He led them to the 1968 league title and into a Super Bowl III matchup with his old team, the Colts. Baltimore was a 17-point favorite (meaning most people thought the Colts would win by at least that much) and few gave the Jets much chance. However, Ewbank and star quarterback Joe Namath guided the Jets' team to a 16–7 vic-

■ *Ewbank (right) beams with QB Johnny Unitas.*

tory—perhaps the most important Super Bowl win ever. The victory established the AFL as a league worthy of respect and gave it more respect entering the merger of the two leagues in 1970. Ewbank is the only coach to win NFL and AFL championships. He was named to the Hall of Fame in 1978.

---

for every team. Carrying the football into the end zone or catching it while in the end zone registers as a touchdown (and six points) for that team. End zones at NFL stadiums are often painted a different color than the rest of the field or may be decorated with team name or logo. Orange pylons at the front corners of the end zone are part of it; players with the ball who hit it score a TD,

Extra point

After scoring a touchdown, a team may attempt a placekick from the two-yard line. If the kick is successful, the team gets one point—the extra point. The play is officially called the "point after touchdown" or "PAT," but is almost always referred to as the extra point. Teams can also run or pass for a two-point conversion.

Facemask

Every helmet has a facemask, which is the term used for the bars that protect a player's face. Made from a combination of rubber and plastic, the facemask is connected by bolts on the helmet located near the ears of a player.

■ *The NFL's plastic-covered metal facemask.*

The facemask was first invented in the 1930s to try to limit the amount of broken noses being suffered by players. However, the bolts used to hold the facemask in place were problematic with the leather helmets then in use.

In 1955, Paul Brown and the Riddell Company developed the BT-5 facemask for Cleveland quarterback Otto Graham. Within five years, most players had a facemask. One notable exception was Pro Football Hall of Fame quarterback Bobby Layne, who when he retired in 1962 was one of the last players to play without a facemask. Today, most players have at least two or three bars to protect their face.

Fair Catch

When a player waves his arm prior to catching a punt or kickoff. The player must raise an arm over his head so the opposing team does not touch the player. The rule was implemented to protect punt returners from getting hit while they were looking up at the ball.

If the player is tackled by the opposition, it is a 15-yard penalty against the kicking team. If the player signals for a fair catch, receives the ball, and then runs, the play is whistled dead.

False Start

When an offensive player moves prior to the ball being snapped. Once the offense becomes set, before the ball is snapped, the offense cannot move. This 5-yard penalty usually is called as the result of an offensive lineman rocking forward or backward prior to the snap. In some instances, the loud cheering by a home crowd can make it difficult for a visiting offensive team to hear its quarterback, thus resulting in numerous false start penalties.

Fantasy Football

Anybody can play fantasy football. The term refers to a combination of players drafted by an individual, who then earn points based on the players' success.

Most fans join a league with anywhere from 8-12 people, draft players, and then play a weekly lineup in an attempt to get more points than your opponent.

While various forms of Fantasy Football existed as early as the 1960s, the frenzy did not really pick up until the late 1990s, with the Internet allowing people to play,

Favre, Brett

Brett Favre (pronounced "FARV") is a legend in Green Bay and is one of the most prolific passers in NFL history.

Favre has completed more passes than anyone else in NFL history and ranks second in NFL history in touchdown passes and passing yards. He ranks third in all-time victories by a quarterback, and has started 237 consecutive games, by far the longest streak ever for a quarterback. He is also the only player to win the Associated Press Most Valuable Player award three times (1995-97).

Favre directed the Packers to the postseason in 10 of his first 12 seasons as the full-time starter. He has thrown a touchdown pass in a record 16 consecutive postseason games. The Packers won Super Bowl XXXI, against the Patriots, following the 1996 season, to bring another title to Green Bay. The Packers reached the Super Bowl the following year, losing to the Denver Broncos.

Among his other record-setting achievements, Favre holds the league record for most seasons with at least 30 touchdown passes, 300 completions, and 3,000 passing yards.

Originally selected in 1991 by the Atlanta Falcons, Favre was traded to the Packers. The move was questioned by some at the time, but Favre's rifle arm and knack for winning in college convinced Packers GM Ron Wolf he had made the right choice. In Favre's first full season (1993), the Packers reached the playoffs and within three years the team won the Super Bowl.

■ *The fabulous Brett Favre (4).*

do research, and keep track of their points and players online. More than 12 million people–including NFL players!–played fantasy football in 2006, with the numbers growing annually. Several kids-oriented Web sites produce free Fantasy Football games you can try.

Faulk, Marshall

Marshall Faulk ranks among the NFL's all-time best pass-catching running backs. Not only was he a 1,000-yard rusher seven times, but he also had five seasons with at least 80 receptions and has more receiving yards (7,185) than any other running back in NFL history. He ranks fourth in NFL annals with 136 career touchdowns and ninth with 12,279 rushing yards.

In 1999, Faulk set an NFL record with 2,429 yards from scrimmage (1,381 rushing and 1,048 receiving). He is also the only player in NFL history to post four consecutive seasons with at least 2,000 yards from scrimmage (1998-2001). The only other two players in NFL history with four seasons (not consecutive) of at least 2,000

■ *Faulk is one of the best all-around backs ever.*

yards from scrimmage are Walter Payton and Eric Dickerson. In 2000, he set a then-NFL record with 26 touchdowns.

Faulk was drafted in 1994 by the Colts and traded to the Rams in 1999. With St. Louis, he helped the team win Super Bowl XXXIV and earn a spot in Super Bowl XXXVI.

Fearsome Foursome

Nicknamed pinned on the Los Angeles Rams' four defensive lineman of the 1960s. Defensive ends Lamar Lundy (with the Rams from 1957-1969) and Deacon Jones (1961-1971), along with defensive tackles Merlin Olsen (1962-1976) and Roosevelt Grier (1963-66), formed the memorable quartet. In 1967, Roger Brown replaced Grier and carried on the tradition through 1969. Jones, a fierce pass rusher who is credited with coining the term "sack," and Olsen, who was selected to the Pro Bowl 14 consecutive times, are in the Pro Football Hall of Fame.

FedExField

The Washington Redskins play their home games at FedEx-Field, the NFL's largest stadium. Located in Landover, Maryland, just outside of Washington, D.C., the Redskins' venue has a capacity of 91,704 fans.

The stadium's first game was

played on September 14, 1997, and was first known as Jack Kent Cooke Stadium, after the team's longtime owner.

Field, the Football

An NFL football field is 300 feet (100 yards) long and 160 feet (53.3 yards) wide. The end zones are each an additional

Fears, Tom

Eighteen catches. Tom Fears had 18 catches in one game. How impressive is that feat? It was an NFL record for half a century. That's right, for 50 years, Tom Fears' name was remembered every time a receiver had a big game and came close, but not close enough, to his record-setting performance.

Fears is the last rookie to lead the NFL in receptions, hauling in 51 receptions for the Los Angeles Rams in 1948. Fears, in fact, is the only player to lead the NFL in catches each of his first three seasons. His 77 receptions in 1949 established an NFL record, and he beat his own mark the following season with 84 catches in 1950, which remained the NFL's best mark for 14 seasons.

■ *Pass-happy Tom Fears.*

The Rams played in four NFL championship games during his nine-year career. In a 1950 playoff game against the Bears, Fears scored all three of the Rams' touchdowns, on catches of 43, 68, and 27 yards, in a 24-14 victory. The following season, Fears caught a pass in between two defenders near midfield and outran the opposition for the game-winning 73-yard touchdown reception as the Rams won their first NFL title since moving to Los Angeles five years earlier. More than 50 years later, his 5 postseason touchdown receptions remains a Rams' playoff record.

Despite his postseason heroics, Fears is mainly remembered for his 18-catch performance against Green Bay on December 3, 1950. Fears finished with 189 receiving yards and 2 touchdowns as the Rams won 51-14.

After his playing career, Fears served as an NFL assistant coach for the Green Bay Packers, where he won NFL titles with Vince Lombardi in 1962 and 1965. He was also an assistant with the Rams and Philadelphia Eagles. From 1967–1970, Fears was head coach of the New Orleans Saints. He was named to the Hall of Fame in 1970.

Carolina's left-footed kicker John Kasay (4) attempts a field goal against the Baltimore Ravens.

30 feet (10 yards) long. The hashmarks on the field are 70 feet, 9 inches from each sideline. The line for extra points/two-point conversion attempts is on the 2-yard line. Logos at the 50-yard line and in the end zone must be approved by the NFL.

Most outdoor fields are played on grass, while games in a dome are played on a variety of different artificial turfs. Every field has a crew of groundskeepers that cut the grass, line the field, and maintain its quality throughout the year.

Field Goal

The term used when a player kicks the ball through the uprights for three points. The kick usually occurs on fourth down, but can take place at any time. The ball is snapped back seven or eight yards to a player kneeling down, called a holder.

The holder stands the ball up and holds it in place with a finger, with the football's laces pointed toward the goal post. The kicker then tries to kick the ball through the uprights while also making sure the opposition does not block the kick.

The longest field goal in NFL history in 63 yards–in 1970 by Tom Dempsey and matched in 1998 by Jason Elam.

If a team misses a field goal inside the 20-yard-line, the opposing team gets the ball on the 20-yard line. If the kicker misses from beyond the 20-yard-line, then the opposition gets the ball at the point of the missed kick.

Field Position

Coaches and announcers commonly talk about the battle of "field position." This phrase is used to describe the importance of a defensive stand or a good punt.

If a punt is downed inside the 10-yard-line, the opposing teams offense is beginning its drive in "poor field position."

In another example, if one team continually begins drives on its own 20-yard-line, while the opposing team is starting its drives near midfield, the latter team would be "winning the battle of field position."

First-and-10

Refers to the down (first) and amount of yards (10) needed for another first down. All possessions by a team, unless it is closer than 10 yards to a touchdown, start with this well-known situation.

First Down

The first play of a new set of downs. First downs can be achieved by gaining at least 10 yards via offense or penalties, or by a change of possession. After a team gains at least 10 yards within four plays, they are rewarded with a new first down, which permits them the opportunity to gain another 10 yards.

Fitzgerald, Larry

As a wide receiver with the Arizona Cardinals,

Larry Fitzgerald has quickly become one of the best pass catchers in the NFL. In 2005, his second season, Fitzgerald tied for the league lead (with Carolina's Steve Smith) with 103 receptions. He became the youngest player (22 years, 123 days) in NFL history to post a 100-catch season. Also, he and teammate Anquan Boldin each had at least 100 receptions and 1,400 receiving yards, becoming just the second pair of teammates in league history to reach those numbers in the same season.

Flag Football

Played by youths and adults internationally, flag football refers to a flag, or similar apparatus, being pulled to "tackle" a ball carrier. Flag football does not need hel-

■ *In flag football, flags (blue and red here) are pulled to end a play.*

mets or shoulder pads, and is a great way for people to play football without having to wear equipment.

Flag football became popular during World War II, as United States military men played games on bases worldwide. Today, flag football is as popular as ever, with more than 100,000 children playing in NFL Flag Football leagues in 2006, with countless more youth and adults enjoying the game on fields across the nation.

Flat

Term used to describe the area of the field where the wide receivers line up. Usually, passes in the "flat" refer to a ball being thrown to a running back who has run over to the space previously occupied by the wide receivers just before the ball was snapped.

The idea of passing the ball into the "flat" is to allow the running back room to

■ *The NFL's official Wilson-made "prolate spheroid."*

operate away from the defensive linemen.

Foolish Club, The

The nickname attached to the original owners of the American Football League. The league began play in 1960, matched in bidding wars with the NFL for college players. Some teams struggled, but all survived. A 1966 merger with the NFL was signed, allowing the 10 AFL teams to be part of the NFL beginning in 1970.

The Foolish Club began when 26-year-old Dallas native Lamar Hunt was foiled in his attempts to bring an NFL franchise to his hometown in 1958.

Hunt contacted others who had shown interest in joining the NFL. On August 14, 1959 the first league meeting was held in Chicago and teams were awarded to Dallas, Denver, Houston, Los Angeles, Minneapolis, and New York. Eight days later, the league was officially named the American Football League.

Football, the

When football first began, around 1869, the football was shaped similar to a soccer ball. A rugby-style ball was used from 1874 until 1912. From there, the ball underwent stages of transformation, until 1934, when the currently shaped football became part of the NFL.

The ball is 11 to 11 1/4 inches

long, and weighs between 14 and 15 ounces. Although it is referred to commonly as a "pigskin," the ball is generally made of steerhide. The ball is made with four panels, which are sewn together. The official shape of a football is a "prolate spheroid."

The only real change to the current football took place from 1956 to 1975, when "night footballs" were used in some games. This white football was easier to

■ *This photo shows players in formation along the line of scrimmage.*

see for players, fans, and viewers. However, the NFL banned the ball in 1976 because the paint on the ball was too slick.

An NFL home team has to have 36 footballs available for an outdoor game, 24 if the game is indoor. There are also 12 footballs used only for kicking. These "K" balls are shipped directly to the officials' locker room and opened two hours before kickoff. The referees check each ball prior to the game to make sure it meets league's specifications.

Formation

A term used for the alignment deployed by an offense or defense prior to the snap of the ball. For example, on offense a team's "formation" may feature

three wide receivers. On defense, the formation may include a fifth defensive back.

Coaches attempt to devise numerous formations, in an attempt to confuse the opposition, both on offense and defense.

Ford Field

Home of the Detroit Lions, Ford Field is located in downtown Detroit and has served as the Lions' home since 2003.

The 64,500-seat, domed stadium served as host of Super Bowl XL in February of 2006, as the Pittsburgh Steelers defeated the Seattle Seahawks 21-10.

Forty-six [46] Defense

A defensive scheme created by Chicago Bears' defensive coordinator

Buddy Ryan and popularized by the franchise's Super Bowl XX title.

Named "46" because of the uniform number worn by Bears' strong safety Doug Plank, the alignment stacked the line of scrimmage with four defensive linemen, three linebackers, and usually the strong safety. Commonly, the defense would over-

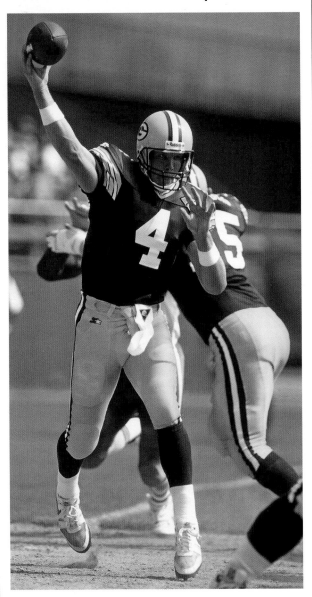

■ *Brett Favre lets loose a forward pass.*

load to one side, with two outside linebackers rushing from the same angle.

Offenses of the 1980s were primarily built to run or use five- or seven-step drops to throw a pass. With the Bears' defense forcing the issue and outnumbering the offensive linemen, opposing offenses were not able to run the ball effectively, nor was their quarterback given enough time to make accurate passes downfield.

In 1984, the Bears' defense set an NFL record with 72 sacks. The 1985 Bears won 15 games and allowed fewer than 13 points per game, by far the lowest in the league that season. In the playoffs, the Bears won 21-0 and 24-0 before defeating the Patriots' 46-10 in Super Bowl XX. In the title game, the Bears' defense recorded a safety, returned an interception for a touchdown, registered 7 sacks, and allowed a Super Bowl-record low 7 rushing yards.

Ryan was with the Bears from 1978 until after the 1985 season, when he was hired as the Eagles' head coach. He took his scheme to Philadelphia, and later Arizona. However, offenses began to counteract the 46 Defense using the West Coast Offense, in which the quarterback makes quick passes after short, three-step drops.

Forward Pass

A forward pass refers to a ball thrown toward the end zone by the quarterback. There are six offensive players that

Fortmann, Dan

A Phi Beta Kappa scholar, Dan Fortmann was one of the youngest and brightest players to ever play the game.

Fortmann was just 19 when he graduated from Colgate in the spring of 1936. At that time, the NFL was holding its first ever draft. For many years, especially at the very first draft, NFL teams did not know much about the college players. It was very possible, even likely, that a team drafted players they had never seen, making the selection only because his name was in a magazine, or because a friend mentioned the player, or a fan wrote a nice letter about his college career. In the ninth and final round of that first draft, with the fourth-to-last selection, Chicago Bears' head coach and owner George Halas selected Fortmann supposedly because, "I like his name."

Halas had to be second-guessing himself when he first met Fortmann. At just 6 feet tall and 210 pounds, Fortmann was small even by Depression-era standards. But at the age of 20, he immediately became the leader of the offensive line, calling out blocking schemes while delivering punishing blocks as a pulling guard. Despite being the youngest starter in league history, he played defense as well (playing "both ways" was done by most pre-1950 stars), where he consistently anticipated plays and was a great tackler. In 1994, Fortmann was selected to the NFL's 75th Anniversary All-Two-Way Team.

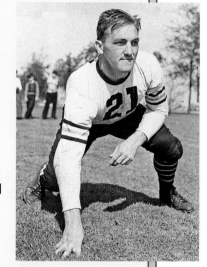

■ *Tough guy Dan Fortmann*

For his eight-year career, Fortmann was selected first team each of his final six seasons in the league, and was a second-team all league honoree the other two seasons. Fortmann helped the Bears win three NFL titles during his career, and finish second on two other occasions. In 1965, he was inducted into the Hall of Fame.

can catch a forward pass, precluding the center, two guards, and two tackles. Yes, the passer can catch his own forward pass if the ball is touched by a defensive player or one of his five eligible teammates.

The forward pass was not a major offensive weapon in the early days of the NFL back in the 1920s. However, in 1929 the football was redesigned to become easier to throw, and by 1934 the ball was approved to its current shape. With passing becoming an option, scoring rose, which led to larger fan attendance.

A team can only make one forward

Foxboro Stadium was home to many great Patriots' moments.

goal in blizzard-like conditions.

Along with Vinatieri's tying kick, another famous field goal was kicked at the stadium. In 1982, Patriots' kicker John Smith kicked a game-winning 33-yard field goal thanks to a snow plow that was used to remove the snow and clear a path on the turf which allowed Smith to plant and kick. This game is referred to as the Snow Plow Game.

pass per play, and the passer must be behind the line of scrimmage. A forward pass is ruled a completion if the receiver has both feet inbounds while maintaining possession of the ball.

Foxboro Stadium

 Served as home of the New England Patriots from 1971 through 2001. The stadium was originally called Schaefer Stadium from 1971-1982 and Sullivan Stadium from 1983-89.

The Patriots won more than 56 percent of their games played at the site, and were 4-1 in postseason games played in the stadium. The last game played at Foxboro Stadium was probably its most famous. In a 2001 AFC Divisional Playoff Game, the Patriots defeated Oakland 16-13 in overtime in a game that is remembered mostly for Adam Vinatieri's 45-yard game-tying field

Frankford Yellow Jackets

The Frankford (Penn.) Yellow Jackets were part of the NFL from 1924-1931, and were awarded the 1926 championship. The NFL did not have a championship game until 1933, so Frankford is credited with winning the league title. The 1926 team had 14 wins (along with 1 loss and 2 ties). The 14 victories were not surpassed for 58 years, until the San Francisco 49ers won 15 games in 1984.

In the 1920s, the NFL's schedule was not designed by the league. Since the state of Pennsylvania did not allow games on Sunday, the Yellow Jackets often played home games on Saturday, then hopped on a train and played an away game on Sunday. Thus the Yellow Jackets played more

Fouts, Dan

The key component of the memorable Air Coryell offense was San Diego Chargers quarterback Dan Fouts.

The first quarterback in NFL history to pass for at least 4,000 yards in three consecutive seasons (1979-1981), Fouts was one of the premier passers in the game's history. Fouts is the only player to ever lead the league in passing four consecutive seasons (1979-1982). In postseason play, Fouts is the only quarterback with four consecutive 300-yard passing games.

Fouts attended the University of Oregon and was a third-round pick by the Chargers in 1973. For five seasons, Fouts was nothing special. Then, during the 1978 season, coach Don Coryell and his high-powered offense changed things.

For the next four seasons, Fouts did not miss a start, and the Chargers made the playoffs each season. Along with wide receivers Charlie Joiner, John Jefferson, Wes Chandler, and tight end Kellen Winslow, Fouts and the Chargers won three

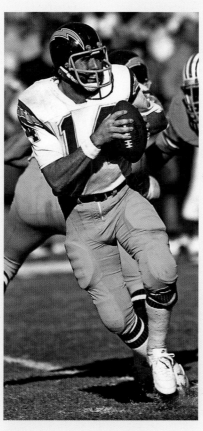

■ *Power passer Dan Fouts*

division titles and led the league in scoring twice.

In 1979, Fouts passed for 4,082 yards as the club finished tied for second in the NFL in scoring en route to a 12-4 record. In 1980, Fouts set an NFL record by passing for 4,715 yards. The Chargers finished 11-5 and fourth in the league in scoring. The following season, Fouts broke his own record with 4,802 yards (which still ranks third all time). In the strike-shortened 1982 season, he was named the NFL's offensive player of the year.

Twice the Chargers reached the AFC Championship Game. In 1980, the Raiders defeated the Chargers 34-27 despite 336 passing yards and two touchdowns by Fouts. The 1981 AFC Championship Game was played in a minus-59 wind chill, which was the lowest in NFL history. The host Cincinnati Bengals defeated the Chargers 27-7.

A six-time Pro Bowl selection, Fouts was inducted into the Pro Football Hall of Fame in 1993, in his first year of eligibility. Today, Fouts is a college football announcer for ABC.

Dwight Freeney is a dominant rusher.

Restricted: Players with three seasons of service and whose contracts have expired.

Transition: Allows the club a chance to match an offer given to the player by another club.

Franchise: There are two versions of franchise players. In the first version, clubs keep an "exclusive" franchise player by committing to a minimum offer based on the averages of the top five salaries at his position. Other clubs cannot negotiate with exclusive franchise players. The second type of franchise player is offered a different sort of offer but may talk with other clubs. His original club may match the offer and keep the player, or receive two first-round draft choices if the original club elects not to match.

Freeney, Dwight

As a defensive end for the Indianapolis Colts, Dwight Freeney is one of the most explosive pass rushers in the NFL.

Freeney is 6-1 and 268 pounds, which makes him one of the smaller defensive ends. Despite his lack of size, the Colts selected him in the first round, with the 11th overall pick of the 2002 draft.

Freeney had 51 sacks in his first four seasons, third best in NFL history, trailing just Hall of Famer Reggie White and Derrick Thomas. Three-time Pro Bowler Freeney had at least 11 sacks in each of his first four seasons.

games (including an NFL record 20 games in 1925–winning 13) than any other team in the league each season from 1924–1930. The Yellow Jackets played their last season in 1931.

Free Agent

A free agent is a player who no longer is under contract with a team. He can talk with the other 31 teams to see if anyone else is willing to hire him. There are four types of free agents:

Unrestricted: Players with at least four seasons of service and whose contracts have expired.

Fullback

The player who lines up in the offensive backfield, usually between the quarterback and the running back. Fullbacks are known primarily for their blocking ability, in which they run in front of the running back to create holes in the defense. On passing plays, fullbacks usually stay in the pocket and help the linemen block oncoming pass rushers.

Some of the better fullbacks of recent seasons include Tampa Bay's Mike Alstott and San Diego's Lorenzo Neal.

Fumble

A fumble occurs when a player loses possession of the ball before the whistle is blown.

Some teams teach their defensive players to try to rip the football out of the ball carrier's hand. Defenses that can perfect this technique can change the momentum of a game. The NFL record for most fumble recoveries in a game is eight, by the Washington Redskins in 1976 and matched by the Pittsburgh Steelers in a 1990 game. A fumble (or an interception) is referred to as a turnover.

■ *Fumble! Kyle Boller loses control of the football, and both teams chase after it.*

Game Plan

The term used to describe the preparation for an upcoming game. The beginning stages of creating a Game Plan are usually within hours of the conclusion of the previous game.

On Sunday night, assistant coaches begin to dissect film of the upcoming opponent. By Tuesday, a complete offensive and defensive scheme have been hatched. The

Gates is one of the NFL's top tight ends.

Game Plan will detail the weaknesses of the opponent, and thus focus on exploiting and capitalizing on their faults.

NFL teams put in countless hours of film study and deliberation before implementing a Game Plan on a weekly basis.

Gates, Antonio

Within the span of two seasons, Antonio Gates became the best pass-catching tight end in football. Not bad for a player who never played a down of college football.

In college at Kent State, Gates concentrated on basketball, but as a 6-4 power forward, Gates did not have enough height for the NBA. Even though he had not played football since high school, the San Diego Chargers signed him in 2003.

As a rookie, Gates finished third on the club with 24 receptions, moving into the starting lineup for the second half of the season. In 2004, Gates made a huge leap, setting an NFL record for touchdown catches by a tight end with 13 and becoming a Pro Bowl starter. In 2005, Gates responded to any doubters with 89 catches. He had 71 catches in 2006.

Georgia Dome

In its first eight years in existence, Atlanta's Georgia Dome hosted two Super Bowls, along with basketball and gymnastics for the 1996 Summer Olympics.

The arena is the largest cable-supported dome in the world and has a translucent roof, made of teflon, that lets in sunlight during the day. The Georgia Dome, which is owned by the state of Georgia, was build solely on money generated from hotel and motel taxes and cost $210 million.

The Falcons moved into the Georgia Dome in 1992 after playing their first 26 seasons at Atlanta-Fulton County Stadium. They won their first two postseason games at the Georgia Dome, 20-18 over the 49ers in 1998 and 47-17 over the Rams in 2004.

The Cowboys defeated the Bills 30-13 there in Super Bowl XXVIII following the 1993 season. In game XXXIV after the 1999 season, the Rams needed a tackle at the 1-yard line as time expired to defeat the Tennessee Titans 23-16 in one of the most exciting Super Bowl games.

"Ghost to the Post"

The name of a famous play that occurred during the 1977 AFC Divisional Playoff Game between the Oakland Raiders and Baltimore Colts.

With the Raiders trailing at Baltimore's Memorial Stadium 31-28 and less than two minutes remaining in regulation, Oakland tight end Dave Casper (nicknamed The Ghost in reference to the Casper the Ghost cartoon) ran a post pattern. Quarterback Ken Stabler lofted the ball deep downfield and Casper made a reaching, over-the-

George, Bill

The first middle linebacker in Bears' history, Bill George was the player who established the incredibly high standard for that position.

George began his career in 1952 as a middle guard on a five-man defensive line. However, in 1954, George, tired of having passes thrown just over his head, moved back a few steps in a game against the Eagles. A few plays after moving himself off the line of scrimmage, he nabbed the first of 18 career interceptions. George is credited with most likely becoming the first middle linebacker in NFL history.

■ *Bill George with his bust at the Hall of Fame.*

George was selected to eight consecutive Pro Bowls during his career. He recovered 19 fumbles during his career. In 1963, he was the kingpin of the Bears' defense that allowed just 10 points per game and won the NFL title, defeating the Giants 14–10. He was elected to the Pro Football Hall of Fame in 1974.

shoulder 42-yard catch at the Colts' 14-yard line. A few plays later the Raiders tied the game, and Casper then made the game-winning, 10-yard touchdown catch in the second overtime as the wild-card Raiders advanced.

Giants Stadium

Home of the New York Giants and New York Jets, Giants Stadium has hosted more NFL games than any stadium in league history.

The Giants used to play playing in Yankee Stadium. They built Giants Stadium in nearby East Rutherford, New Jersey in 1972. Located less than seven miles from Times Square, the new stadium hosted its first game on October 10, 1976. The Jets left Shea Stadium and began to share the site with the Giants in 1984.

The Jets, not wanting to reference another team in their home stadium's name,

▥ The "G" stands for goal line.

refer to their home as The Meadowlands. The stadium is predominantly blue, but for Jets games green banners surround the site. The two teams go so far as to each have a different seating capacity. The field had artificial turf from 1976-1999, grass from 2000-02, and currently games are played on FieldTurf.

Gifford, Frank

Please see page 94.

Gillman, Sid

Please see page 95.

Gillette Stadium

The home of the New England Patriots, who won 26 of their first 32 games there after moving into it for the 2003 season. They are also 5-0 in postseason home games, including a 24-14 victory in the 2003 AFC Championship Game against Indianapolis.

Goal Line

You have to score points to win, and to score points a team must reach the goal line, which runs the width of the field and serves as the last hope for the defense and the finish line for the offense.

The goal line is actually in the end zone. Thus, if a player reaches with the ball and touches any part of the goal line, the result of the play is a touchdown. Along with a line on the field, the goal line is noted with large, orange signs with a bold, black "G" on them.

Gibbs, Joe

Joe Gibbs looks like a professor, and that is exactly what he was while coaching the Washington Redskins for many seasons.

Gibbs was the coach of the Redskins from 1981–1992, winning four NFC championships and three Super Bowls. He took a 12-year break in order to run a NASCAR auto team, and then he came back to coach the Redskins again in 2004.

Gibbs was 40 years old when he took over the Redskins in 1981. His team lost its first five games that year and finished 8-8. But in 1982, the Redskins won the NFC title as well as Super Bowl XVII.

In 1983, Gibbs' team was back in Super Bowl XVIII but lost to the Oakland Raiders.

Four years later, in 1987, Gibbs had the Redskins in the Super Bowl again, this time with a happy ending. Washington routed Denver 42-10 in Super Bowl XXII.

In 1991, Gibbs' Redskins were the most dominant team in the league, finishing 14-2, and winning Super Bowl XXVI.

Gibbs' three Super Bowl victories were notable in that they were done with three different starting quarterbacks—Joe Theismann, Doug Williams, and Mark Rypien. Gibbs retired in early 1993, and in 1996 he was enshrined in the Pro Football Hall of Fame.

■ *Gibbs returned to the Redskins in 2004.*

Gibbs retired from football, but not from sports. He managed the Joe Gibbs Racing Team in NASCAR for the next 11 years, winning dozens of major races.

He was often approached by NFL owners about returning to coaching, but he turned them all down until 2004, when he accepted a $25 million offer to return to the Redskins at age 63. In his second season, 2005, he had the team in the playoffs again, only this time Washington lost in the second round.

Gibbs always was known as a workaholic whose days often ended at midnight and began at dawn. Winning was hard work. The old professor just made it look easy. – J. W.

Gifford, Frank

While many fans today remember Frank Gifford only as a former announcer of Monday Night Football, he was actually one of the best players of his era.

Gifford joined the New York Giants out of the University of Southern California in 1952. A runner, receiver, and defensive back, he was one of the NFL's last two-way players. The Giants played in five championship games during his career, winning the 1956 title. In that season, Gifford combined for 1,422 yards from scrimmage and was unanimously selected the league's most valuable player.

In 1960, Gifford got tackled by Eagles linebacker Chuck Bednarik. Gifford suffered a concussion and missed the remainder of the season. He then retired in 1961, only to come back in 1962 as a wide receiver. He had seven touchdown receptions each of his first two seasons as a wide receiver, claiming a Pro Bowl selection at a third different position (defensive back, running back, and wide receiver).

After his playing career, Gifford did some acting in movies and began a long run as a football announcer, first for CBS and then on ABC's Monday Night Football, where he stayed for 23 years. Gifford was selected to the Pro Football Hall of Fame in 1977.

■ *Gifford leaps into action.*

Goal-line Stand

Refers to a defense stopping a team multiple times within a few yards of the end zone. Goal-line stands are often game-changing plays. Most goal-line stands involve a defensive line coming together to stop a charging running back or quarterback trying a sneak. But they can also involve stopping pass plays, too.

The most famous Super Bowl goal-line stand took place in Super Bowl XVI, when the 49ers played the Bengals. After three plays from inside the 49ers' 3-yard line, the Bengals went for a touchdown on fourth-and-goal. Linebacker Jack Reynolds and cornerback Ronnie Lott stopped Pete Johnson for no gain, giving the ball back to the 49ers, who held on to win 26-21.

Gillman, Sid

Few men left larger impressions on football than Sid Gillman, who coached in four decades beginning in the mid-1950s.

The game we watch today—with wide-open passing and multiple action—is the game that Sid Gillman pioneered when he joined the Los Angeles Rams in 1955. We call it the West Coast Offense. Gillman simply saw it as a way to move the football.

He began coaching at Miami of Ohio in 1944, in an era in which running the ball was thought to be the surest way to victory. Gillman disagreed.

"The big gains come with the pass," he said. "If you want to ring the bell, you have to pass."

Gillman brought that philosophy to the NFL with the Rams, leading Los Angeles to the Western Division championship in 1955, his first season. He left the Rams in 1959, but landed a job coaching the Los Angeles Chargers of the AFL in 1960.

The Chargers moved to San Diego in 1961, but they continued to stay at the crest of the AFL, playing in five of the first six AFL Championship Games, winning only one, in 1963 over the Boston Patriots.

Gillman led the Chargers until 1969. He had an 82-47-6 record in a decade with the Chargers.

In 1973, Gillman became the general manager of the 1-13 Houston Oilers. He later briefly coached the team.

Over the next 20 years, he continued to

■ *Gillman's ideas on offense were revolutionary.*

consult with numerous teams, including the 1980 NFC-champion Eagles.

In addition to the West Coast Offense, Gillman is widely recognized as the modern innovator in the use of game film. He was elected to the Hall of Fame in 1983 and died at 92 in 2003. — J. W.

Goal Posts

Goal posts are the vertical poles located at the back of each end zone; players kick the ball through the uprights for one or three points. NFL goal posts are bright gold and stand 18 feet, 6 inches wide. The crossbar which connects the posts is 10 feet off the ground, and the posts are at least an additional 30 feet high. The ribbon attached to the top of each post allows the kicker to gauge the wind.

Into the 1970s, the goal posts were H-shaped and located on the goal line. The NFL moved the goal post beyond the end zone in 1974.

Gonzalez, Tony

Tony Gonzalez is the second-leading tight end pass catcher of all time, and also ranks second in receiving yards and Pro Bowl berths, trailing only Shannon Sharpe in all three categories. He is one of three tight ends (Ozzie Newsome, Browns, and Sharpe, Broncos) to own a franchise record for career receptions.

In 2004, Gonzalez established a tight end record for single-season receptions with 102. With his 102-catch season, Gonzalez led the league in receptions, becoming just the third tight end to accomplish that feat (Kellen Winslow, Chargers, 1980

Goodell, Roger

On August 8, 2006, Roger Goodell was named the NFL's eighth commissioner. Goodell began his football career as an unpaid intern many years earlier, so it completed quite a trip.

Goodell replaced Paul Tagliabue, who had served as commissioner from 1989-2006. Goodell began working with the NFL under then-commissioner Pete Rozelle back in 1982, and by the 1990s was one of Tagliabue's most trusted advisors. In 2001, Goodell was named the NFL's chief operating officer. Among his many duties were stadium construction, expansion, and overseeing the NFL's businesses and officiating. Goodell also played a key role in the negotiations for a labor contract agreed upon by the owners and player's union in March of 2006.

Goodell takes over one of the biggest jobs in sports. As commissioner, he is responsible for everything about the league, from scheduling games to planning television contracts. The team owners run their teams, but the commissioner runs the league.

■ *The NFL's man in charge.*

Graham, Otto

Quarterback Otto Graham's nickname was "Automatic Otto." He never missed a game in his 10-year pro career, and his Browns teams played in 10 of 10 possible championship games and won seven titles.

Graham began making a mark on the first day of his life and never stopped. He weighed 14 pounds, 12 ounces at birth, an Illinois state record. The son of music teachers, he was the state French horn champion at age 16. As a high school senior, he was all-state in basketball and football. In college at Northwestern, Graham was All America in both basketball and football in 1943.

Graham signed with Cleveland's new AAFC team in 1946 and led the Browns to

■ *Otto Graham was a winner.*

four straight league titles. He also played for the 1946 NBA-champion Rochester Royals.

Graham and the Browns moved into the NFL in 1950. Cleveland was 12-2 during the regular season, then defeated the Los Angeles Rams for the NFL championship.

The Browns lost the NFL title game each of the next three years before winning the 1954 championship. Following the game, Graham announced he was retiring. He came back at the start of the 1955 season and led the Browns to another title. In his final game, Graham and the Browns beat the Rams for the 1955 NFL title.

"The test of a quarterback is where his team finishes," Browns coach Paul Brown said. "By that standard, Otto Graham was the best quarterback of all time." Graham died in 2003. — J. W.

and Todd Christensen, Raiders, 1986).

Gonzalez primarily played both football and basketball at the University of California before the Chiefs chose him with the thirteenth overall selection in 1997. Listed at 6-5, 251 pounds, Gonzalez uses his power forward skills on the basketball court to help gain separation from defenders and give the quarterback a good target.

Grant, Bud

Bud Grant is one of only a few people who played in both the NFL and the NBA. It was in the NFL, however, that he had his greatest success. As head coach of the Minnesota Vikings, Grant led his teams to 168 wins, one NFL championship, and three NFC titles.

After his playing career ended, he

Grange, Harold (Red)

Harold (Red) Grange was football's first rock star. He was the biggest name in college football at the University of Illinois from 1923-25, and his legend grew to epic levels when he graduated to pro football.

No one before him—or, for a long time after him—matched his colossal achievements.

■ To this day, Red Grange remains an NFL hero.

➤ After Illinois, the dazzling running back, known as the Galloping Ghost, signed a contract for more than $100,000—an unheard-of total then and comparable to multi-millions today—to play a series of exhibitions from coast to coast with the Chicago Bears.

➤ On the tour, Grange attracted record crowds wherever he went, including 100,000 in Los Angeles and 80,000 in New York. In Miami, the suburb of Coral Gables built a 40,000-seat wood stadium in four weeks just for him, filled it for the game, then tore it down and built a housing development with the wood.

➤ He was the first football player to sign product endorsement deals (for, among other things, cereal, candy, soap, cigarettes, pencils, and typewriters), and he was the first to star in movies (his first was a blockbuster, *One Minute to Play*).

➤ Grange was so big in 1926 that he and the Bears could not agree on an NFL contract. Owner George Halas offered Grange a one-third share of the Bears' team, but Red turned it down. Grange and his business manager, C.C. Pyle, then started their own league, the American Football League (AFL), with Grange as the star of the New York team. Grange's team played at Yankee Stadium and was called the Yankees.

In this NFL-AFL war, the NFL won after one year when the AFL folded. But there was a victory of sorts for Grange. His Yankees were added to the NFL in 1927.

From 1928-1935, Grange was back in a Bears' uniform, teaming with fullback Bronko Nagurski to help Chicago win NFL titles in 1932 and 1933. Grange was only 32 when he retired in 1935. In 1963, when the Pro Football Hall of Fame first opened, Red Grange, the "Galloping Ghost," was one of the first 17 men selected to join. — J. W.

coached in the Canadian Football League for 10 seasons and won four league championships. Joining the Vikings in 1966, he led them to their greatest successes. They won 10 Central Division titles in 11 years.

The strength of Grant's teams was a defense known as the "Purple People Eaters," which finished in the top three in fewest points allowed seven times in an eight-year span from 1969-1976. Five times, Grant's team lost just two games in a 14-game season. In other words, the Vikings dominated the regular season for much of the 1970s.

The Vikings reached the Super Bowl four times in an eight-year stretch (1969-1976), a feat matched only by the Dallas Cowboys (1971-78, 1972-79), Pittsburgh Steelers (1974-79), and Buffalo Bills (1990-93). Grant remained the Vikings' head coach through 1983, and then came back for one more season in 1985.

He was the first person to be inducted into both the Pro Football Hall of Fame (1994) and the Canadian Football League Hall of Fame (1983).

"Greatest Game Ever Played"

Despite being an overtime thriller, the 1958 NFL Championship Game is called the "Greatest Game Ever Played" not because of its on-field excellence, but due to the long-term impact it had on football as a televised sport.

The game featured the Baltimore Colts and New York Giants at Yankee Stadium. The NFL, in 1958, was a 12-team league with two six-team divisions, and trailed baseball and boxing in popularity. That was all about to change.

The Colts, led by future Pro Football Hall of Fame quarterback Johnny Unitas, drove 73 yards in the final minutes to set up a game-tying field goal, and Baltimore then drove 80 yards in overtime, capped by Alan Ameche's 1-yard run, to defeat the Giants 23-17. The game was the first overtime game in NFL history, and had by far the largest television ratings in football history.

In 1955, NBC paid the NFL $100,000 to broadcast the championship game. When the next contract came out in 1961, that fee had jumped to $615,000. In 1962, CBS agreed to pay the NFL $4.65 million annually for all of its regular season games. By 1965, the Harris Poll determined that football had surpassed baseball as America's most popular sport. And in 2006, four television networks paid the NFL $3.1 billion annually for all of their games. Much of football's popularity can be attributed to the 1958 NFL Championship Game.

Gregg, Forrest

Vince Lombardi is considered probably the best coach in NFL history. So who was the "finest player" he ever coached? Forrest Gregg.

Green Bay Packers

With the most NFL championships, its legacy of great players and coaches, and the fact it is a publicly-owned team with by far the smallest television market in the NFL, the Green Bay Packers are one of the league's most storied franchises.

The Packers have the second most members (20) inducted into the Pro Football Hall of Fame, including coach Vince Lombardi, wide receiver Don Hutson, and quarterback

■ *Bart Starr was the Packers' longtime QB.*

Bart Starr. The 1996 Brett Favre-led Packers won Super Bowl XXXI, giving "Titletown USA" its 12th NFL championship.

Green Bay was a semipro team which, in 1919, accepted $500 from the Indian Packing Company for its uniform and equipment. The team became the Packers, and joined the NFL in 1921, the league's second year. After missing a year in 1922 due to rules violations, the club became a publicly held company in 1923. Led by coach Curly Lambeau, the club became the first to win three consecutive titles (1929-1931). In 1933, to ease their money problems and tap into a larger market, the Packers began playing some of their home games in Milwaukee, a tradition they continued through the 1994 season.

In 1935, the Packers drafted Hutson, who led the league in receiving eight times (nobody else has led the league more than five times). Green Bay won NFL titles in 1936, 1939, and 1944. Lambeau guided the club to six titles before retiring in 1949.

The Packers' home, Lambeau Field, first opened in 1957. It has served as one of football's most historic fields. In its 50th season in 2006, Lambeau Field was the longest continuously occupied NFL stadium, and ranked third among all pro sports, trailing just baseball's Fenway Park and Wrigley Field.

In 1959, the Packers hired Vince Lombardi and promptly posted their first winning record (7-5) in 12 years. The next season, the club reached the NFL Championship Game, where it lost to the Philadelphia Eagles. With Lombardi's coaching excellence, and the play of Hall of Famers such as Starr, running backs Jim Taylor and Paul Hornung, linebacker Ray Nitschke, defensive end Willie Davis, and defensive tackle Henry Jordan, the Packers won five of the next seven NFL titles, capped by victories in Super Bowls I and II.

Super Bowl I was not only a key game for the Packers, but for the NFL's respectability. The American Football League, or AFL, had begun in 1960. By 1966, it had forced a merger with the NFL. Lombardi's Packers did not let the NFL down, posting a 35-10 victory over the Kansas City Chiefs, followed by a decisive 33-14 win against the Oakland Raiders the following January.

Lombardi retired from the Packers after his second Super Bowl in 1967, and the Packers posted just five winning seasons in the next

25 years. In 1992, the Packers made three key personnel moves. First, the board of directors hired Ron Wolf as general manager. Wolf signed San Francisco 49ers' offensive coordinator Mike Holmgren as head coach, and then traded his first-round rookie pick to the Atlanta Falcons for their second-year reserve quarterback, Brett Favre.

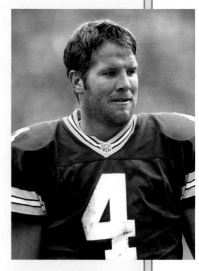

■ *QB Brett Favre led the Packers to Super Bowl XXXI.*

Favre came off the bench in the third game of 1992, rallied the club to a victory against Cincinnati with a last-minute touchdown pass, and the Packers had their quarterback for the next 15 years. Favre ended the 2006 season among the leaders in several all-time passing categories. Defensive end Reggie White signed with the club in 1993, and the Packers reached the playoffs 10 of the next 12 seasons, highlighted by a 35-21 over the Patriots to win Super Bowl XXXI.

GREEN BAY PACKERS

CONFERENCE: NFC

DIVISION: NORTH

TEAM COLORS: DARK GREEN, GOLD, AND WHITE

STADIUM (CAPACITY): LAMBEAU FIELD (72,922)

ALL-TIME RECORD: (THROUGH 2006): 648–514–36

NFL CHAMPIONSHIPS (MOST RECENT): 12 (1996)

Greene, Joe

He was known as "Mean Joe" Greene, a nickname that only represented the man on the field, where he dominated a defense from his defensive tackle position.

Greene was the first pick of the Pittsburgh Steelers in 1969 and was the NFL defensive rookie of the year. With Greene on board, the Steelers began building a dynasty.

Greene was named the NFL's defensive player of the year in 1972 and 1974. The 1974 Steelers reached Super Bowl IX, defeating the Minnesota Vikings 16-6 with Greene contributing with an interception and fumble recovery, for Pittsburgh's first-ever Super Bowl title. The Steelers proceeded to win Super Bowl's X, XIII, and XIV, as well.

■ *He was only "Mean" if you had the football.*

With 10 Pro Bowl berths, Greene was the best defensive tackle of the 1970s. He retired after the 1981 season, and was later selected to the Hall of Fame.

Despite being slightly undersized at 6-4 and 250 pounds, Gregg played in 188 consecutive NFL games, then a league record, and played in nine consecutive Pro Bowls. He was renowned for watching film of the opposition, learning every one of his opponents' moves

In 1959, Gregg's second year with the Packers, Lombardi led the team to the NFL Championship Game.

The Packers also won NFL titles in 1962, 1966, and 1967. The latter two championships placed the Packers in Super Bowl I and II, where they were victorious in both games. In 1971, Gregg joined the Dallas Cowboys for one final season. The Cowboys won Super Bowl VI, and Gregg retired as a six-time NFL champion.

After his playing career, Gregg immediately went into coaching. Within three seasons, he was head coach of the Cleveland Browns (1975-77). In 1981, under Gregg, the Cincinnati Bengals reached Super Bowl XVI, where they lost to San Francisco. Gregg coached in Cincinnati through 1983, and then took over his old team, the Packers. He guided the Packers for four seasons.

Gregg was selected to the Pro Football Hall of Fame in 1977 and was on the NFL's All-Time 75th Anniversary Team.

Gridiron

Another term for a football field, it was first used in the *Boston Herald*

newspaper in 1897 while describing the Harvard-Yale game.

The origin is based on a cooking grill sometimes being referred to as a grid iron, with its metal, parallel bars. From high above, a football field has yard lines every five yards that look like bars, which look like a grid, leading to the term "gridiron."

Guard

A position on the field, the guard lines up on the offensive line next to the center. There are two guards, a left guard and right guard, on the field at all times. The guards' main job is to protect the quarterback on passing downs, while creating holes in the defense for running backs on rushing plays.

Groza, Lou

For many years, Lou "The Toe" Groza was the NFL's all-time scoring leader. A strange statistic indeed for a player who was a nine-time Pro Bowl player at tackle. Groza was both a star offensive lineman and the Browns' kicker. He played 13 seasons as a starting tackle, but also spent all 21 of his seasons kicking for the Browns.

In 1946, Groza was primarily a kicker his first season as the Browns won the All-American Football Conference title. He became a starting offensive tackle in 1947. With the Browns, Groza won three more AAFC titles, along with three NFL titles. In 1950, after joining the NFL, Cleveland posted a 10-2 record, and it was Groza's 16-yard field goal in the final seconds of the 1950 NFL Championship Game that gave the Browns a 30-28 victory and an NFL title in their first season in the league. He led the NFL in field goals five times during the 1950s, and in 1954 *The*

Sporting News selected Groza as the NFL's Player of the Year. He retired in 1960 with a then-NFL record 1,349 points in the NFL.

"The Toe" was elected to the Hall of Fame in 1974. Today, the top college football kicker each year is given the Lou Groza Award.

■ *"The Toe" tees off.*

*Read the index this way: "**4**:62" means Volume 4, page 62.*

National Football League

NOTE: *The numbers following a team's name indicate the volume and page number where the information can be found. "I:36" means Volume I, page 36.*

American Football Conference

East Division		North Division		South Division		West Division	
Buffalo Bills	I:36	Baltimore Ravens	I:24	Houston Texans	II:16	Denver Broncos	I:64
Miami Dolphins	II:70	Cincinnati Bengals	I:50	Indianapolis Colts	II:24	Kansas City Chiefs	II:38
New England Patriots	II:86	Cleveland Browns	I:54	Jacksonville Jaguars	II:32	Oakland Raiders	III:4
New York Jets	II:92	Pittsburgh Steelers	III:28	Tennessee Titans	IV:62	San Diego Chargers	III:56

National Football Conference

East Division		North Division		South Division		West Division	
Dallas Cowboys	I:58	Chicago Bears	I:46	Atlanta Falcons	I:20	Arizona	I:14
New York Giants	II:90	Detroit Lions	I:66	Carolina Panthers	I:42	St. Louis	III:54
Philadelphia Eagles	III:24	Green Bay Packers	I:100	New Orleans Saints	II:88	San Francisco	III:58
Washington Redskins	IV:90	Minnesota Vikings	II:74	Tampa Bay Buccaneers	IV:54	Seattle	III:66

About the Authors

James Buckley Jr. is the author of more than 60 books for young readers on a wide variety of topics—mostly sports! He has written several books on football, including *Eyewitness Football, Eyewitness Super Bowl,* and *America's Greatest Game.* Formerly with *Sports Illustrated* and NFL Publishing, he is now the president of the Shoreline Publishing Group, which produced these volumes.

Jim Gigliotti was a senior editor at NFL Publishing and the editor of the league's national GameDay program. He has written hundreds of articles on football for many magazines and Web sites, as well as several children's books on other sports topics.

Matt Marini was also an editor with NFL Publishing, where he oversaw the *NFL Record & Fact Book* among many other writing and editing duties.

John Wiebusch is one of America's leading experts on pro football. As the vice president and creative director of NFL Publishing, he was the editor of the Super Bowl program for 32 years, and author and/or editor of thousands of articles on all aspects of pro football. John is the author of *Lombardi* as well as dozens of other books, and has edited more than 200 titles. He also wrote a popular NFL history column on AOL. He contributed numerous essays on Hall of Fame personalities in these volumes.

DATE DUE

OCT 1 3 2009		
OCT 2 7 2010		
JAN 0 4 2010		
JAN 2 4 2011		
OCT 2 8 2011		
MAY 28 '12		

The Library Store #47-0152